NO LONG
SEATTLE

D0501336

THE GILDED RAGE

THE GILDED RAGE

A Wild Ride through Donald Trump's America

ALEXANDER ZAITCHIK

Hot Books

Copyright © 2016 by Alexander Zaitchik

All rights reserved. No part of this book may be reproduced in any manner without the express written consent of the publisher, except in the case of brief excerpts in critical reviews or articles. All inquiries should be addressed to Skyhorse Publishing, 307 West 36th Street, 11th Floor, New York, NY 10018.

Hot Books may be purchased in bulk at special discounts for sales promotion, corporate gifts, fund-raising, or educational purposes. Special editions can also be created to specifications. For details, contact the Special Sales Department, Skyhorse Publishing, 307 West 36th Street, 11th Floor, New York, NY 10018 or info@skyhorsepublishing.com.

Hot Books® and Skyhorse Publishing® are registered trademarks of Skyhorse Publishing, Inc.®, a Delaware corporation.

Visit our website at www.skyhorsepublishing.com.

10 9 8 7 6 5 4 3 2 1

Library of Congress Cataloging-in-Publication Data is available on file.

Cover design by Brian Peterson

Print ISBN: 978-1-5107-1428-1
Ebook ISBN: 978-1-5107-1430-4

Printed in the United States of America

Contents

For Haydée, Fabiola, and Juanita

The more those elitist eggheads shouted, "The Dead Are Walking," the more most real Americans tuned them out.

— Max Brooks, *World War Z:
An Oral History of the Zombie War*

*Do you know so much that you call the slave or the dullfaced ignorant?
Do you suppose you have a right to a good sight . . . and he or she has no right to a sight?
Do you think matter has cohered together from its diffused float, and the soil is on the surface and water runs and vegetation sprouts for you . . . and not for him and her?*

— Walt Whitman, *Leaves of Grass*

Foreword

The opinion class in this country has been so wrong for so long— blowing it badly on the Iraq War, the crash of 2008, the growing crisis in race relations, the "inevitable wisdom" of the new global economic order, and nearly every other major issue—that it came as no surprise when these experts also failed to get the significance of the Trump uprising. The media elite initially greeted Trump with glee, as an uproarious ratings and circulation boon, a showman who would soon give way to the next circus act. When instead he pulled off an unfriendly takeover of the Republican Party, the media giddiness turned to fear and loathing. But as the mood of the media elite shifted suddenly from merriment to panic, little light was actually shed on the meaning of Trump. By focusing almost exclusively on the strangely hued candidate himself—and exposing his manifold flaws and eccentricities—the media establishment clearly hoped to restore reason in the land. But our professional explainers have once again failed to understand the popular bitterness and rage underlying the Trump phenomenon—a fury that is directed in no small part at elites like them, and that will continue to burn long after Trump has disappeared from the spotlight.

So it comes as a relief to read independent journalist Alexander Zaitchik's report from Trumpland. As he criss-crossed America, going to the political rallies, bars, and diners where Trump supporters gathered—and sometimes being invited into their homes—Zaitchik was not setting out to *explain* these men and women who so confound the political commentators but to *listen* to them. *The Gilded Rage* gives these voters a chance not just to spit out a sound bite or two but to express themselves at length. These are the discarded veterans of the endless wars in the Middle East, the blue-collar workers who will never again match the money they made when they were young, the residents of rural hamlets and suburban outposts that are always overlooked by the media radar. They emerge in this book not as bigoted and ignorant caricatures but as people with deeply legitimate grievances and with riveting stories about the underside of the American Dream.

This is the kind of probing and surprising journalism that Hot Books was intended to showcase. Launched in 2015 in partnership with Skyhorse Publishing, Hot Books offers an ongoing series of short, powerful titles on the most burning topics: the fragility of black lives in America (*The Beast Side*), the campus rape crisis (*The Hunting Ground*), the moral and legal challenges presented by post 9/11 US war crimes (*American Nuremberg*), the untold story behind the Edward Snowden case (*Bravehearts*), the dangerous rise of Islamophobia (*Scapegoats*), and the CIA's subversion of the media (*Spooked*), among others. We see Hot Books as part of the great revival that is now starting to spread across America and the world, as long sluggish democracies begin to rouse themselves. These books are meant to provoke and to spark debate. Please spread the word—use them in your book clubs, classes, and social media forums.

It's time to light a fire under this slumbering giant, American democracy. It's time to think new and dangerous thoughts. Welcome to Hot Books.

David Talbot
Hot Books Editorial Director

THE GILDED RAGE

Introduction

"Who *Are* These People?"

Twenty-sixteen has been a disorienting political year for us all. Insurgents stormed both party establishments in primary-season offensives that few saw coming. The Democratic fortress held, but just. The Republican castle burned, and how. A real estate warrior king in orange face paint arose from the east and sacked it, backed by a long-simmering internal revolt. Nobody knows yet what this sacking portends. The party could absorb Donald Trump or deflect him; it could disappear altogether in the rubble of a high-Richter realignment. We do know there's no going back. Months before completing his GOP body count on a May evening in Indiana, Trump had blown the old order and its stale wisdoms sky-high. Bits and globs still rain down across the land, nowhere harder than greater Miami, where they splatter on the political headstones of Jeb Bush and Marco Rubio.

This book is not directly about any of that. It's not about how Donald Trump humiliated the Republican establishment, turned presidential debates into high-stakes roasts, or represents the deathbed gasp of American democracy. Trump is the looming and unifying presence, but this book is not really about him. It is about the everyday Americans who love, support, and believe in Donald Trump, who see him as a savvy patriotic businessman and tough-talking savior, the last hope for reviving the blue-collar middle class and getting America back to being "great," a Rorschach-blot adjective many Trump critics read as "white," and which many fans read as "a place with decent jobs, tight borders, and please stop calling me a fucking racist."

For Trump voters, too, this has been a disorienting year. But theirs is a giddy disorientation. After decades of mounting disaffection with both parties, they can't believe they scaled the castle walls and now have a chance to hang the last Clinton with the guts of the last Bush. Even better, they get to follow a brash celebrity who talks like Andrew Dice Clay and says exactly what they feel and (they hope) means every politically incorrect word: about trade, the vets, Social Security, Mexicans, Muslims, busty broads—about so many things.

The disorientation that hatched this book was not the giddy kind. Last winter, I watched with anxiety as Trump racked up victories and packed rallies modeled on the politics and spectacle of monster truck shows. There was plenty to fear in the rest of the GOP field, but Trump alone built his political profile by hawking Birther theories on *Fox & Friends*. He alone called for a Muslim travel-ban and spoke wistfully of General Pershing's apocryphal fondness for shooting Muslim combatants with bullets dipped in pig's blood. Only Trump wrote recipes for national greatness in horror fonts, such as his call to harness America's medieval ingenuity behind a torture program targeting the wives and children of suspected terrorists. Then there was the Great

Wall, Trump's signature policy idea and defining campaign metaphor, promoted with racist insults.

Like Jeff Goldblum in *The Fly*, Trump entered the race having completed a dangerous experimental mutation, from gossip-page guppy and playboy developer, to a new breed of rightwing populist, equal parts Howard Stern and Michael Savage, Tony Robbins and Father Coughlin, Kim Kardashian and Benito Mussolini. The pundits and pollsters assured us the experiment would fail, that this 200-pound insect-man bioengineered by Joe McCarthy's old lawyer would be dead within weeks. According to their calculations using the laws of Beltway physics, Donald Trump was not possible. In a Republican primary, a candidate could not attack John McCain for his war record and survive, any more than an orange floats to the ceiling after rolling off a table. But a funny thing happened on the way to the Bush-Kasich ticket. Trump's mutant organs not only functioned, they grew stronger, feeding off the energy of millions of Republicans and conservative Democrats. Where many saw a monster, these voters saw a lovable superhero. They loved him for his braggart wealth, his dramatic renderings of browbeating the CEO of Carrier Air Conditioners, for his merciless taunting of media and political elites, for telling the Bushes where they can stick their land wars and trade deals, for defending Social Security and Medicare, for packaging a hopeful story of industrial decline and renewal in the language of a realtor-turned-infomercial pitch man ("*Unbelievable* people, *terrific* people, used to work in these factories").

Trump's breaks with Republican orthodoxy gave some of his enemies on the left pause, but never overrode the loathing and confusion. In the cities and neighborhoods where I spend most of my time, Trump hatred is a given, as is the belief that his supporters deserve the same, whether it's expressed in media ridicule or eggs thrown at their faces as they enter Trump rallies. The sentiments expressed about these Trump voters might be boiled down to the rhetorical question, "Who *are* these people?"

Stripped of condescension, this is a good question. A more difficult, more interesting, and more important one than, "Who is Donald Trump?"

It was with this question—"Who are these people?"—scribbled atop an empty notebook that I joined the campaign trail midway through primary season, in Phoenix. My plan was simple, inspired by the late Studs Terkel: sit down and talk to Trump voters. Or, as Terkel would say, listen to them. For the next three months, I traveled six primary states conducting long-form biographical interviews with Trump supporters. A fraction of those interviews make up most of the following pages. They have been edited for length and clarity, and mortared with scene reporting for context.

I met my subjects in different places, mostly in bars and the parking lots of Trump events. With some people, I spent several hours, with others, several days. Some invited me to their homes. Our conversations always got around to politics, but rarely started there. Mostly we talked about their lives, their formative experiences, what it was like growing up in their corner of the country. These things are also the stuff of politics, just not the kind that can be easily quantified.

The long-form interviews that make up the heart of this book are as far as you can get from the stat-and-poll driven journalism that failed so spectacularly this year, and that has never felt more insufficient or unsatisfying. It's also the far side of the room from punditry and "hot takes" written by people living several time zones and income brackets away from their subjects. In April, *New York Times* columnist

David Brooks, the consummate Beltway-creature bore, confessed a flash of self-awareness by promising to make occasional excursions from his northern Virginia suburb "out into the pain" to meet some of the seventy-five percent of Trump voters who say their lives have steadily gotten worse over the last five decades. Brooks didn't mention the roles he and his fellow pundits have played in this pain, but shaking its hand and looking it in the eye is a good place to start.

What did I find in Trump country? Most of the people I met seemed to me fundamentally decent people. Some were decent, but with slightly enlarged spleens. Others were just plain nasty. Still others, well, people are complicated. I don't dismiss the studies showing higher than average "authoritarianism" and racism among Trump voters, but I didn't observe very much of it. (The raging sexism around Hillary Clinton is another story.) However much I disagreed with them, or winced at their Archie Bunker diction, or mourned the telltale signs of Chronic Talk Radio Syndrome, I could almost always find seams of empathy under the bluster. Many working-class Trump supporters are dependent on some kind of government program or subsidy, or know somebody who is. Yet they've generally worked hard in their lives, and they don't like being denigrated as "takers." I was often surprised by how easily their pride blended into a (sometimes grudging) generosity toward the very downtrodden groups Trump is famous for attacking. It's possible they were dissembling. There's no accepted margin of error for honesty, especially with a recorder on the table. But I believe the average Trump voter resents condescending elites many times more than he even thinks about brown people, and cares more about the local unemployment rate much more than national demographic trends.

Among the Trump supporters I got to know well—dozens during three months on the road—few of them took Trump's most outlandish ideas literally. When asked about the Wall or mass deportation, most shrugged them off as metaphors for getting serious about the border. Not a few have a fine appreciation for the spectacle of it all. They know Trump is in the WWE Hall of Fame; they made popcorn for *The Apprentice* as well as his GOP debate smackdowns of "Lyin' Ted" and "Low-Energy Jeb." Often their cynicism runs deep enough to suspect the whole thing is just another giant set-up: they cheer and jeer, their opponents seethe, and somewhere out over the horizon, Les Moonves and Joe Scarborough are clinking Arnold Palmers on a private beach in the Hamptons.

Even if Trump exits stage right in November, the widespread disaffection and anger he's harnessed and inflamed will continue as the star of the show. At the start of the second George W. Bush administration, the big question on the left, formulated by Thomas Frank, was why conservatives couldn't snap out of the GOP's culture war trance. Now Trump voters have answered it, but in a way that reminds us to be careful what we wish for. Frank sees Trump as the "the crude and ugly reflection" of the Democrats' failure to answer his question first. I'm not sure that a populist Democratic platform could provide a bridge over some very deep cultural rifts, but there's no option but to try. The alternative is a future where something else is the matter with Kansas, something we've just begun to glimpse, but still feels like a specter. Not for nothing does media around the world put Trump in the same frame as the ethno-nationalist, far-right parties surging across the model welfare states of Europe.

No group of interviews can divine the meaning or gauge the threat of Trump's rise. The answers will unfold with time, delivered by the three hundred million citizens of a diverse and troubled continental empire. Who are these people? Here are some of them, presented as a small group self-portrait, composed during a moment of national disorientation. Take from it what you will.

Oakland, California
June 2016

Chapter One

Arizona

Trudging the sidewalks of Fountain Hills, it was easy to fall in emotionally with the parade of Trump supporters. No one was happy about walking three miles in the sun. Wearing weather-inappropriate jeans and socks, I was maybe unhappiest of all. I knew my near future involved chafed thighs and ointments, and this knowledge put me in tune with the chorus of conservative complaint: *Liberals don't have any arguments, so they block traffic. . . . This is what welfare people do—make chaos and ruin the weekends of people who work for a living. . . . I heard it was mostly Latinos that blocked the road—why didn't the police stop them when they drove in?*

It was a fair question: What's the point of passing the nation's gold standard in Nurembergian racial-profiling legislation if you can't prevent a caravan of activists from wreaking havoc in Sheriff Joe Arpaio's own damn suburb?

On Saturday morning, four days before the March 22 Arizona primary, protestors formed a blockade of parked cars on the road leading to an outdoor Trump rally co-starring Arpaio and former governor Jan Brewer, the state's twin icons of the immigration hardline. Arpaio's deputies towed the cars and arrested three anti-Trump protestors. They then blockaded both entrances to the adobe-themed Scottsdale suburb of Fountain Hills, turning back cars and directing everyone to park along the sandy blacktop shoulders of Highway 87. The resulting migration looked like the parking lot trek to a desert music festival, maybe one that culminated in the symbolic burning of a giant wooden Mexican.

Early into the walk I met Danny Riggs, an affable Scottsdale native, Trump supporter, and recent Georgetown University graduate. Riggs was twice angry: about having to walk in the heat to hear his candidate speak, but more about his mother, a Fountain Hills resident whose home had been enclosed by protestors and police blockades all morning. The inconvenience, he said, had accomplished something the team efforts of her son and husband could not. It had pushed Mrs. Riggs into Trump's camp. "My mom wasn't sure about him before all this, but now she's into it," he told me. "She's getting a T-shirt and everything."

I told him there was debate on the left about the ethics and strategy of trying to shut down Trump events. Some veteran activists said roadblocks and shout-downs were right and necessary expressions of dissent against nascent fascism; others found them contrary to principle and ultimately counterproductive. "Oh, guaranteed," said Riggs, the protests would only bring in more recruits like his mother.

"The protestors say Trump is dividing the country, but they're the ones stopping us from exercising our rights. We came to see a conversation. Now we're an hour late. Trump's late. We're walking two and half miles. My car's parked on the freeway. A group of protestors blocks you in your own home? I'm not saying 'violence', but I'm sorry, you'd be shot for that in a lot of states."

It's not clear if Riggs meant "states" as in the Nutmeg State, or nation states. Before I could clarify, Trump's motorcade rolled past us toward the rally grounds. At its center was the black SUV containing the candidate and Arizona Governor Doug Ducey, fresh from a live-audience recording of Fox News' *Hannity* at the Phoenix Convention Center. Arpaio had joined them onstage, but left early to oversee rally security in Fountain Hills. (Two months later, in response to the anti-Trump protest, Ducey would sign a bill increasing penalties for blocking access to a campaign event.)

"There they go," said Riggs, gesturing at the motorcade. "That's them, if you want to tape it, or something."

I dutifully held up my phone and took a picture, but the only thing worth recording about Trump's Arizona limousine was the backseat conversation he shared during his visit with Arpaio, the celebrity sadist-avatar of his immigration platform, whose eighty-three-year-old grip, Arizonans had begun to murmur, ain't what it used to be. Did Sheriff Joe, serving a sixth term on the slimmest electoral margin of his career, coach Trump on how to navigate the demographic winds and federal boulders that menace the highways and back-ways of immigrant bashing? Did he share *Cosmo*-style tips on How to Arouse the Fiery Maricopa County Republican Lurking Inside Every Moderate East Coast Retiree? More likely, the student had become master and Trump had nothing to learn from Arpaio.

If the candidate needed any tutorials from his Arizona friends, it was help in understanding why everyone kept bringing up that dead Arizona senator with the Jewish name, the one with the thick glasses, who once dropped a Trump-sized turd in the Establishment punch bowl, sending packing Nelson Rockefeller, the Jeb Bush of his day, only to get crushed by the Democrat in November, because everyone pretty much agreed his election would set in motion events culminating in a global thermonuclear holocaust.

The ghost of Goldwater haunted Trump as his caravan entered the view of Arpaio's snipers. Both the widow and son of the legendary conservative had recently unloaded on the candidate in the media, calling him a "cowboy" and an "authoritarian." But those were genteel put-downs next to the protest signs greeting Trump in Fountain Hills Park, not a few of which invoked Hitler by name. A fenced-off rally area was set up near an artificial lake featuring the giant geyser that gives Fountain Hills its name. Between it and the rest of the rolling, sixty-acre park, a long white wedding tent shaded dozens of police in tactical vests. Above it all in a sky of cloudless blue hovered enough police choppers to monitor an uprising in a major city.

I arrived at the park in a sweat, just as Trump took the podium, his voice dying against a white noise of dueling chants. The loudest duel had Trump fans screaming "U-S-A!" against protestors screaming "Trump Is Hate!" The three-syllable scream-offs mixed menace with a comic undercurrent, as the scene called to mind the classic Miller Lite showdown . . . "Taste Great! Less Filling!" Roving packs of pros and antis grew and shrank as people gathered, drifted off, and took breaks after going hoarse. Some of the screaming contests winnowed into dyads, leaving two people so far in each other's faces they looked more likely to French than fight. Amplified snatches of Trump's speech poked through: *Build the wall . . . End Common Core . . . Smart trade . . . George Patton . . . End Obamacare . . . The CEO will call me in ten minutes . . . Rebuild our military . . . Win with the military . . . Winning . . . So much winning . . .*

Throughout Trump's speech, passions, including what felt like a hot and burning hatred, rose, spread. Was this going to be The Day? The kind of day remembered as Bloody Saturday, or the Arizona Beer Commercial Riots? The biggest story in the country was the atmosphere of violence that had defined Trump's recent campaign events. Not a week before, an event in Chicago had been cancelled after street scuffles broke out. Rumors swirled of a nascent Trump militia called the Lion's Guard, raising the prospect of Trump brown shirts retailored in Red, White, and Blue. But there were ghosts closer to home than Nazi Germany, such as the American Legion gangs who attacked left-wing activists and union halls during the Great Depression, and later acted as muscle for the "Americanism" movement of Joe McCarthy. Fountain Hills seemed too posh a venue for knuckle politics, but this was Arizona, a border state where immigration is personal. There were pieces in place for some kind of mayhem. Both sides had numbers. There was plenty of space. The police were hanging back. A bloody afternoon brawl felt possible.

The pot steamed and never boiled. After the speech, Trump supporters drifted off with more chants and parting comments, including, "Go back to Mexico" and the "The entitlements office is that way." But drift off they did. One guy who'd been bellowing "U-S-A!" at the top of his lungs in protestors' faces walked over to his antagonists and said quietly before leaving, "You guys do know that you're fucking idiots, right?" Some of the scream-offs cooled into something resembling conversations. I saw two men go from the brink of fisticuffs to a bonding session over their shared revulsion for Ted Cruz and Hillary Clinton.

Later that afternoon a similar script played out in Tucson, Trump's final Arizona event before the voting: road blockade, chanting, confrontations, chest bumping, but no blood. That protest may have minted a few more Trump supporters like Danny Rigg's mom. After returning from the rally, a black Tucson police officer named Brandon Tatum posted a public video chastising protestors for being aggressive and "hateful" toward rally goers. Tatum's video threw fuel on the Left's smoldering in-house debate over how to protest Trump, how and whether to engage his supporters, and the ethics and efficacy of trying to stop his events from taking place altogether.

* * *

On Monday, the day before the primary, I took a long city bus ride up Cave Creek Road, passing roughly seven hundred sad strip malls, to Trump's Arizona headquarters. The operation was located in a two-story office complex set behind a McDonald's on the bleak outskirts of North Phoenix. It wasn't much: two modest rooms with a dozen two-person tables for phone banking. The scene was quiet, the energy flat. The campaign staff were in their early to mid-twenties, mostly from outside the state. The volunteers averaged a few decades older, mostly over fifty and all white, with the exception of a tiny Latina woman who came with her husband, a tall taciturn fellow in a cowboy hat.

I had come to get a feel for Trump's Arizona operation, such as it was. A preppy-shaggy male staffer from New Orleans set me up with a headset and call-list. "Just try and stick to the script and let me know if you have problems with the system," he said, in a friendly but dickish manner suggesting the former presidency of a large Southern fraternity.

Arizona is a closed primary, so I spent the day telling registered Republicans about the importance of voting for

Donald Trump, "the only candidate who will put America first." Most people I spoke with had already voted early for Trump. A few hung up on hearing Trump's name, but not many. One woman sounded to be trembling in anger when she said, "I will *never* vote for that man." One guy said he wanted to like Trump, but was deeply troubled over the candidate's breach with his favorite Fox News personalities. "Listen," he told me. "You need to sit down with your candidate and tell him he needs to straighten up and fly right. He's way off base going after Megyn Kelly."

For several hours, I shared a table with Lynn, a talky sixty-something New York transplant in khakis and a yacht club polo shirt. She knew Trump was going to win Arizona, but worried about establishment shenanigans behind the scenes. "Who is counting the votes?" she said. "That's the question. I don't trust John McCain. He's a snake." She didn't trust the media, either, and was curious to gauge my knowledge of anti-Islam sentiment in Europe. "The French just had another huge protest against the Muslims. They don't want 'em. But you didn't hear about it in the media. It's like a communist country!"

At lunchtime, a Domino's deliveryman walked in carrying a stack of pizzas, care of the campaign. As he entered the room, Lynn demanded to know if she could count on his vote on Tuesday. "Well, uh, I'm really more of a Bernie guy," he stammered, setting down the pizzas and backing slowly away like someone who'd just taken a wrong turn into the egg chamber in *Alien*. Lynn jumped. "A Bernie guy! So the pizzas must be *free*, right? I hope nobody *paid* for these pizzas." The joke met with silence, so she loudly explained it. "Get it? They're *communist* pizzas, so you don't have to *pay* for them. You just get them *for free*."

Lynn left after lunch and was replaced by Gracie, a subdued soccer mom type who spoke in a whisper that made everything sound like a secret. "You know, this Cuba trip?" she said to me in a hush between calls. "Obama taking his *whole family* to Cuba? He says his daughters are interested in this and that, but you know it's just another vacation. That's all it is." Later, she asked me if I knew that Obama was trying to give himself an eighteen percent raise. "Can you believe it? A raise for all ex-presidents. For the *rest of their lives*. Trump won't need to do that," she said. "He's already rich."

The next morning, primary day, I went back for the final push. Terrorists had just bombed the airport and a street corner in Brussels, and I expected to find the room buzzing with talk of tactical nukes and mushroom clouds forming over territory controlled by the Islamic State. During an interview with the *Washington Post* the previous morning, Trump had refused to rule out going nuclear. But nobody at Trump's Phoenix HQ seemed to care or even know about the Brussels attacks. At the coffee and donut station, the volunteers, now including a young black woman named Toni, were still talking about Saturday's rally in Fountain Hills. My tablemate, a retired advertising executive from Chicago named Nancy, remained in shock over the lack of mass arrests. "I can't believe they didn't arrest them all," she said. "They just towed the cars away! I took pictures of the protestors and offered them to the police. They did nothing. To be honest with you, I was a little surprised at Sheriff Joe."

Nancy had ideas of her own for making America great again. "I think people should have to pay an income tax to vote," she told me. "Except maybe old people. Maybe they're too poor or whatever." She also prided herself as being something of an amateur historian. Trump's recent speech to The American Israel Public Affairs Committee (AIPAC) had been a tour de force, she said, but little-known historical forces ensured it would be lost on American Jews. "I did a study," she explained. "I used to be confused that my Jewish friends were so liberal. So I researched it. It's because back in the 1880s, after all the pogroms, the Jewish industrialists, Guggenheim and Singer and guys like that, they funded all these kibbutzes in Israel, which were communist. And now, people still hear about it from their grandparents."

It was around then that I excused myself, thanked the staffers for the coffee and donuts, and left to catch the bus downtown. Waiting at the bus stop, in the bright heat of the Arizona afternoon, I found myself staring longingly at a dive across the street. The hand-painted sign on the wall commanded me: "Be Wise, Socialize . . . At Larry's. Relax, Bring A Friend If You Have One." I followed the order and walked over to have a much-needed drink. The place was mostly empty; a klatch of older day drinkers sat glumly at one end of the bar. On the other side, my side, sat a large, tatted up, bandannaed man in his thirties with a beer gut and a goatee. His sleeveless leather biker jacket read "Independent Wounded Veteran" in gang script across the back; a patch on the front read, "Heroes don't wear capes, they wear dog tags."

The TV in the corner had on news about the election. I pointed at the screen. "You got a dog in this fight?"

"Trump. I voted for Trump," he said. "He doesn't have a bazillion different backers funding his shit. We need to bring big business back and not outsource so much. Every time Trump opens his mouth it helps him. He's not scared of putting his foot in it. He is able to say, 'You know what, I might not have said it the right way, but this is what I want to do.' I like that he isn't sure if he wants to be a Republican or a Democrat. Who cares? He's got something to bring to the table, and enough testicular fortitude to do it. I like that he's got balls and he's willing to take a chance. Not taking a chance hasn't worked too well."

Over a few rounds of Bud Light, I learned that the man, a native Phoenician named Anthony Holston, had a special issue: the Veterans Health Administration. Veterans' issues drove his vote the way guns or taxes drove other voters. A disabled Army vet, Holston had served in Kosovo, Afghanistan, and Iraq, where he was wounded by an RPG and took two bullets. He returned to Phoenix from Baghdad in 2005 plagued by a raft of chronic physical and psychological injuries, including PTSD. The most important institution in Holston's life was the local VA hospital. He had no love for the politicians who sent him to war only to come back to what he described as a dysfunctional and underfunded VA system.

When Trump criticized John McCain—Arizona's seeming senator for life and famed Vietnam POW—for not being a "hero," pundits in D.C. thought it a mortal error that spelled game-over for his insurgency. But in Arizona biker bars like Larry's, it helped lock up the votes of vets dependent on Arizona's scandal-plagued VA system. Trump may be an overgrown New York rich kid who dodged Vietnam like the rest of his brat pack, but no candidate talks more about veterans' issues. Holston jolted to attention when he heard Trump bluntly state vets were "living in hell." He'd never heard a candidate say that before. It was a fact both true and personal. Holston's younger brother, Dominick, killed himself after he returned from Iraq with PTSD.

Holston also cheered when Trump insulted Jeb Bush and broke a party taboo by accusing George W. Bush of lying to sell the Iraq War. "Trump was right," he said. "Bush Jr. was trying to clean up for his daddy and their friends. They were all in business together. They all still own shit over there. They're making money off of our fucking loss.

And the ones that lost are going further and further in the fucking hole."

Holston was eager to talk about the depths of this hole. "It's hard to work because I drink all day to deal with what I went through," he said. "I did what I had to do over there, what they told us to do, but some things . . . . I can't look at my kids sometimes. I've lost four wives. One night I woke up in a cold sweat after my ex-wife hit me with a broomstick. I was choking her out. Then you go down to the VA, and they give you anti-depressant pills that make you a zombie, and they go, 'You're good.' The pills make me stupid. I'm not a stupid person. I'd rather drink. It's the only way I can fall asleep. My back is in constant pain. The VA only gives me ibuprofen. I take my mom's Percocets so I can move around and function. It's a horrible life."

I recognize the Slavic word for "family" tattooed down the length of Holston's right forearm—*Rodzina* in block script— and ask him about the surrounding images spilling out from under his black T-shirt.

"Everything on this arm has got to do with my family. They came forever ago to Ellis Island from Warsaw. For holidays, we still do sausages and perogies, spinach with soft pork, sour cream. This knife and scabbard is for my dad. He was a master chef. The bell is my mom, born Christmas Eve. Here I got my kids' names with a rattle and pacifier. They are my true love. Here, my little bulldog, that looks like poop. That's me and my brother. The Phoenix, because I am from Phoenix, born and bred.

"I grew up in the same house that I'm at right now, in the mobile home complex right here off Thirty-second Street. It was my grandma's house. When my grandpa passed away, she was like, 'I'm moving to Arizona where it's no more snow.

I don't want to deal with that crap anymore.' I'm the first generation born in Arizona. My family is all from Michigan.

"I'm a white boy that's always worked. I was laying carpet, tile, and wood flooring at twelve. I learned trades young. But I was stupid. In high school the cops were pulling me over by name. It was like, 'I either end up in jail or I got to do something.' So I joined the military with my brother, Dominick. He was a Marine. I was Army. We'd just graduated high school.

"When 9/11 happened, I was in basic at Fort Knox. They pulled everyone into formation and said, 'We're being attacked. Here's your M16, here's your rounds.' This was week six, out of eight. Graduation day. Goddang! Eighteen years old. Young, dumb, and full of cum. Ready to fire guns. After Basic, I did Kosovo first, a peace mission, played fricking gate guard. I watched Russian soldiers shove glow sticks up dogs' butts and use them for nighttime target practice.

"My unit was one of the first into Baghdad. I was a mechanic and spent six days at Camp New York just to make sure our vehicles were lock, stock, and ready to roll. During a desert maneuver, rounds started flying. They said, 'Get in your vehicles, we're rolling now.' I dropped my spade and went straight through the berm [anti-tank embankment]. Everybody followed. That was March of '03. Taking Baghdad was a lot different from what you saw on TV [*laughs*]. A lot of the Iraqi soldiers we met were trying to give up. They'd run out butt-naked, saying, 'We've got no gear on, no nothing!' If the Iraqi soldiers in uniform caught them, they'd roll them in concertina wire, prosecute them on the spot. Judge, jury, and executioner.

"I damn near died at the Baghdad International Airport, Saddam International, whatever you want to call it. We were the first ones there and got ambushed. Took two RPGs to the back of my M88A2 Hercules—a big ass track vehicle, a huge target, super slow. The motor blew up and my hatch slammed shut on my spine. I couldn't run, couldn't move. My flack vest stopped two bullets at the bone.

"From then on, I was in excruciating pain. The field medic can help with broken limbs and shit, but all they tell you is take two Tylenol. It sucked, but you're working off pure adrenaline. For eight months, I was a mechanic extraordinaire, did anything that needed to be done. I think our battery had the fastest motor-swap time in the battalion. We could replace a motor in like twelve minutes. When you're getting shot at, it seems like an eternity. The pain kept getting worse. I'd tell the hospital, 'Tylenol is not cutting it. I can't run. You're not looking at the problem here.' It's been that way ever since. Nobody wants to do anything about it. It got so bad I had to find a way out. I got fat. Gained a bunch of weight until I couldn't do anything. I got a Chapter 13 [disability discharge].

"All that shit over there, it brings you to here, and four marriages [*trails off, pauses*]. Coming home, I was scared shitless. My family was in Vietnam, Korea, WWI, WWII. They came back womanizers and killers. I said, 'I don't want that shit.' I started having nightmares everyday. I see the kids. . . . There were things over there we did that were . . . unexplainable. When you get told to . . . seven-year-old kids. Do or die, you gotta do what you're told, if an NCO tells you to do it, guess what? Don't do it, and you get in more trouble, or you die. I look at my kids. . . . They're the same age as some of the kids over there.

"When my brother got back, he got messed up in the head, ended up committing suicide. There was like eight guys in his unit that were threatening to commit suicide, and my brother talked them down. He grew up to be a real good guy. I'm a little bit more stubborn than he was. My brother was the pushover, lawyer type. I'm more of the rough-and-tough type. I will do what is necessary to survive.

"I got to be a really bad drunk. Real bad. After my third wife walked out on Christmas morning, I turned myself into the VA. For being psychotic. I spent five days trying to kill myself in my backyard by running my head into a block wall. I'd pass out and my dog would wake me up. Roxie. An old English bulldog. She is pretty much the only reason I stayed alive. She'd lick me and clean up the wounds on my forehead and I'd go back to drinking again and getting stupid again.

"They put me in a padded room for twenty-four hours. Put me on pills. I started going through counseling. Then the counselor left, and I was right back at square one. You finally get to a point where you can talk to somebody, and they leave. I don't trust a whole lotta people. I let things go for a while. My ex got custody of the kids and moved to Canada. That tore me up and I realized I had to fight for my kids. Now I've got two of them full time. I try not to . . . get stupid until after they are asleep and I can have my issues in my room.

"For a long time, I didn't know it was possible to get help. You try to Google anything about the VA—it's a runaround. You end up getting even more pissed off, more of an angry vet [laughs]. I finally started filing paperwork at the VA in September of 2010. It took almost three years for me to get anywhere with them, to get a disability rating, to get any kind of help. It took three years. Now, once a year, they test me for anything under the sun, chemical related.

At this point, Holston's girlfriend, Jessica Garcia, entered the bar and sat down next to Holston. She had short-cropped hair and wore a leather biker vest with a patch that read, "I support my veteran." Holston explained who I am and why there was a recorder on the bar. "Cool," she said. "I'm a Trump girl, you can talk to me, too."

"The first time I had to call the psych help line, he was in the tub trying to drown himself. They said, 'Oh, well what's his primary doctor?' I don't know anything. I said, 'His name is Anthony Holston. He is in the system, can't you look him up?' There was no help at the VA. Like, four times the past year, he comes out more pissed off because they're not doing anything, just giving him stupid pills."

I brought up some experimental drugs that I knew were being used with success to treat veterans for PTSD, including ketamine and MDMA. Holston was upset that he'd never heard about the trials.

"If something is working, why aren't we trying that? Why aren't we doing something? I'm going to ask them about that. If John McCain was forced to use the VA for his medical care, shit would change. But guys like him go to the Mayo Clinic and have private doctors. There is a song by System of a Down. It goes, 'Why do we always send the poor?' When I was in Iraq, some politician was in the news saying he would never send his sons over. What are we? Little pawns in your fucking game? Your son is important, but nobody else is? Bullshit. People with money get away with murder. You don't got money? You're fucked. An $8 minimum wage? Are you serious? What are you going to get for $8 hour out here? What do you actually take home a week?

Garcia jumped in: "When all the Mexicans and everybody were fighting for $15, I was working at McDonald's. That one right there, right across the street. I'm kind of on the fence about that. I'm thirty-two. I've done McDonald's since I was sixteen. I've worked at fifteen different McDonalds all over Phoenix. In a sense, it would be nice if McDonald's workers could make $15 an hour, but there has to be stipulations on it.

If you're making $15 an hour, you should be with McDonald's for more than five years. You should have the training. You don't have to be a manager. Just be there for five years."

I asked Holston what he thinks of Trump's foreign policy views and the ban on Muslims. "We gotta stop going to war with countries and paying them billions and trillions of dollars. Let's fix our own. What country out there would blow our shit up, and then pay us? 'I know we just blew up like trillions of dollars worth of your buildings and everything, but let me pay you back.' Who does that? [laughs] We're the only ones.

"I don't think the ban [on Muslims] should be permanent. Let's put a ban on certain things that we know are happening. No international flights right now, sorry for you, but they want to fight in Belgium, they're wanting to fight over here. Sorry, none. Get on a fucking boat. Trump wants to build a border wall. Let's do it. Let's stop spending all the money on all the people [entering the US illegally]. We're not a melting pot anymore. Look where that got us. But illegals are going to be illegals, you're going to have them no matter what you do. They find a way in. And they're the ones willing to walk behind elephants picking up elephant ass. I respect that. I also respect how they're family oriented. Mess with one, you mess with the whole burrito. That's how I was raised.

"Since we're never going to get rid of all of the illegals, why focus on it? If you don't make it an issue, then it is not an issue. If you focus on the bad, that's all you have is bad. Start focusing on some good: let's get big business back, more work, higher wages, lower unemployment, and if you've got a higher minimum wage, we're not going to have so many people on welfare eating up our taxes."

This got Garcia's blood up. "My ex-husband has a girl-friend. She's had thirteen goddam kids, and the only reason why she makes it every month is because she has DES [Arizona's Department of Economic Security]. And she's a fucking Mexican."

"Well, she's a single mother with thirteen kids who are all under the age of eighteen," interjected Holston.

"She's a single fucking mother with thirteen fucking kids because she can't keep her goddamn legs closed," Garcia shot back. "I had one child. I get $62 a month in food stamps. That's it. I put more than that in gas in my truck. Instead of spending a trillion dollars on a wall, put it into DES. I can't afford health insurance for myself, then I get fined when I pay my taxes. Obamacare is bullshit."

"Obamacare hurt everybody," agreed Holston. "I honestly think we should adopt Canada's fucking type of health care system. Everybody pays $130 a month, you've got healthcare no matter if you're rich or poor. Age, race, nothing, it doesn't matter, everybody pays the same $130, that way there is no discrimination, clear across the board. Everybody gets the same kind of coverage. Everybody gets taken care of. This system sucks. My mom and dad paid $4,900 a month for insurance. My dad's been in the hospital for weeks. They treat him like he's an underprivileged, illegitimate fucking nothing.

"People also need places to live," continued Holston. "There's halfway houses for vets all over the fucking place. Up in Flagstaff, my buddy's uncle started a tent farm. It's like a big tent farm for vets. If they've got nowhere to go, no food, no shelter, they can go up there, they've got tents already set up with fucking sleeping beds. It's all volunteer. They go up there and they can crash out in tents and enjoy the good weather and get fed. They've got food and everything out there. It's a hella cool thing, man.

"There was a guy downtown that was trying to do it on a piece of property, further downtown by, like, the central

Phoenix area. He got fuckin' ix'nayed by the Council. The City Council just shut him down. He had tents and everything up, and was like, 'It's my property. I will do what I want.' And they were like, 'No, you won't. It's unsanitary.' It wasn't. He hosed everything out, cleaned it well.

"There are programs for homeless vets, but most homeless vets are old. They don't have smart phones to get on the Internet and find it. Vets aren't getting taken care of. How many suicides a day? It's ridiculous. All it takes is somebody to talk to."

When I left the bar later that afternoon, Holston and Garcia were holding hands with one arm and lifting a fresh round with their other. Holston didn't look like a grizzled vet with demons so much as a teenager over the moon with his first girlfriend. He looked at the floor and blushed when Garcia told me in parting how proud she was of him for speaking with me. "He never talks about this stuff," she said. Later that night, Trump won Arizona by twenty-two points.

Chapter Two

Wisconsin

"This awesome awakening—the shifting and—sifting and—the exposing of—this rabid—bite for them to—hang on to—any kind of relevancy—and to hang on to their—gravy train . . ."

Some found refuge in wadding napkins. Others fiddled with their forks, swirling scraps of fried fish and mashed potatoes. A few covered their faces with their hands. Those with eyes open traded furtive, knowing looks with strangers. A gray-haired woman at my table squeezed her husband's arm and quietly said, "She's hurting him more than she's helping him." Less quietly, someone else said, "Oh, my God."

At the front of Milwaukee's Serb Hall, framed by a Patton-sized American flag, Sarah Palin stood talking to a couple of thousand Wisconsin Republicans. She was speaking on behalf of Donald Trump, who'd declined an invitation to join his rivals and address the fish fry. His snub didn't surprise

anyone. The night's line-up was thick with the same local officials and talk radio hosts who for months had been tag team-
ing a concerted statewide Trump beat-down. With Ted Cruz
way up in the Wisconsin polls, Trump dispatched Palin to
this hostile den of GOP badgers, the state mascot that looks
cute in pictures but is really a vicious, razor-clawed preda-
tor. In this way the animal is a lot like the façade "Wisconsin
nice." The same polite, *Fargo*-accented Republican Party the
national media said was "turned off" by Trump's brusque
demeanor was one of the leanest and meanest in the country.

Speaker after speaker at Serb Hall reminded the audience
of their knife-cold accomplishments: theirs was the party
that cut benefits and neutered public sector unions, passed
a voter ID law to reduce minority and student turnout, and
beat back a historic recall attempt aimed at the leader of this
miserly movement, Governor Scott Walker. In the words of
Vicki McKenna, the local talk radio host who emceed the
Serb Hall event, "We're different. We're a beacon on how to
do government."

As Palin crashed around the stage on verbal stilts,
it seemed possible that she was Trump's revenge on his
Wisconsin tormenters, the easiest way to ruin their fish fry.
If so, it worked, at least a little. Next-day press accounts noted
the lack of applause during Palin's speech, but none captured
the variety of tortured expressions that blossomed as Palin
spoke in a cadence that sounded less like a stump speech
than a testimonial presentation on the dangers of long-term
methamphetamine and alcohol abuse.

Palin's shuttle disaster at Serb Hall was of a piece with the
Trump caravan's Wisconsin arrival in the state. In Arizona,
a desert state on the Mexican border, Trump strutted to victory on an official red carpet. Wisconsin was all windswept
contrast, a gray and snow-dusted planet of fish fries and

shitty poll numbers, populated by disciplined and austere conservatives living on a moose-patrolled Canadian border. Governor Walker, the battle-scarred Koch Brothers yes-man, endorsed Ted Cruz just as Trump Force One touched down in Milwaukee, but only after making cryptic comments suggesting that he enjoyed private fantasies about a contested convention, a white horse, and a smoky hotel suite in Cleveland. Pundits promised it all added up to the firewall they'd been hallucinating since Iowa. *Washington Post* columnist E.J. Dionne assured readers, "This time it really is the end of Trump. Really."

Trump would lose Wisconsin as expected. But even among the middle-class, suburban party leaders who populated the Serb Hall fish fry, the after-dinner conversation at my table suggested there was more Trump support than was indicated by the wall-of-silence response to his surrogate from Alaska. Seated to my right, a twenty-something salesman named Mike Reynolds announced the evening had only deepened his loathing of Ted Cruz. He was voting Trump. This admission caused less of a stir than his praise of the outgoing Democratic president. "Is Obama really so bad?" he asked the table. "I mean, my 401K doubled. The stock market has doubled. The only thing I really don't understand, is why is he so easy on Islam?"

Across from Reynolds, a straight-backed middle-aged man in rimless glasses and a sharp nose sprang to life. "Obama—*not so bad*? Ha! He destroyed the economy," he said. "Business confidence, the real estate market—they collapsed after his election. Overnight. His policies—*retarded*. Just retarded." The man introduced himself as Dennis Vlach, an area landlord and award-winning realtor for RE/MAX. He declared his own fierce allegiance to Trump, the Wisconsin GOP be damned. "I'm disappointed in them," he said.

I made plans to meet Vlach for breakfast later in the week. But first there were Trump events to attend, including a rally in West Allis, home of one of Wisconsin's most iconic economic ghosts, the old Allis-Chalmers industrial plant, which once employed twenty thousand workers building tractors and turbines for the world, and is now a parking lot.

* * *

Talk to locals over forty, and they'll tell you stories about when Milwaukee—today the fourth-poorest city in the country and one of the worst hit by the foreclosure crisis—was a manufacturing boomtown. Trump's bare-knuckled talk of "smart trade", tariffs, and bringing back the old days was tailor-made to appeal to those on the losing end of the state's decline. Not that he had any competition. At Serb Hall, his rivals made only brief rote gestures toward the area's cratered industrial economy. Ohio Governor John Kasich said he understood Trump's gut appeal to many blue-collar workers. "You're angry," he said. "You're upset about this or that agreement." But he did not criticize these agreements, which he had backed, shifting instead into a paean to Reaganomics. Likewise, Ted Cruz made an emotional appeal for the votes of "the men with calloused hands." But it too was an appeal without mention of outsourcing, declining wages, or job-killing trade policies—global capital developments beloved by Cruz's friends at Goldman Sachs.

The next morning, many of these "men with calloused hands" packed a hall to see Trump in Racine, an old red-brick industrial city midway to Chicago along the shore of Lake Michigan. I arrived early to find the auditorium already filled to capacity. The downtown streets were busy with disappointed Trump supporters walking back to their cars. Opposite the venue, a couple dozen protestors chanted, "Trump is hate!" behind a police line. They shivered against biting winds whipping off of the lake, which seemed to change color by the minute: flat and sleet under cloud cover, to tropical aqua under the sun. One protestor bemoaned, "This is a pathetic showing. We should be ashamed."

On Main Street, I joined a bearded older man in a Trump cap who was handing out Trump stickers and little handmade cards to passing cars and pedestrians. One side of the card listed the people and organizations that opposed Trump— Soros, the UN, Black Lives Matter. The other side featured a YouTube logo and a website address beneath the words, "Paul Harvey: Our Lives, Our Fortunes, Our Sacred Honor." The man, a retired Texas veteran named Mark Spence, was on a mission. He'd been following Trump through several states, getting to know fellow Trump supporters and trying to revive an audience for Paul Harvey, a folksy radio personality beloved by generations of conservatives before his death in 2009.

"I haven't felt a fellowship like this in a long time," Spence told me. "It's something special. I'm having the time of my life." Behind him was the white Ford pickup he'd been living in during his travels through Florida, Texas, Utah, and now Wisconsin. Spence wasn't worried about the American people, he said. They would elect Trump as the GOP nominee, and then as president. What worried him was a counterattack by elites to shut down the democratic process. "I keep waiting to turn on the radio and hear that they've suspended welfare payments," he said. "That will start a crisis in the cities. There won't be any election then."

Later that afternoon, I met Spence a second time in the parking lot of West Allis High School, not far from the old Allis-Chalmers plant. As in Racine, thousands were already in line several hours before doors opened. It was a target-rich afternoon for the vendors who trawled the queue barking their wares like hot dog vendors at a baseball game: "T-shirts, hats, buttons!" A half dozen of them were on the trail full-time, living off a political merch version of the old Grateful Dead parking-lot drug-and-tie-dye economy. Several worked both Trump and Bernie rallies. "They buy the most stuff," said one traveling vendor. His top-selling Trump items were two buttons: "Bomb ISIS" and "Hillary For Prison 2016."

I joined the line and fell into conversation with a local couple and their teenage daughter. Kathy, the mother, was a friendly woman with bright red hair. When I mentioned I was a reporter, she told me to turn on my recorder. "I'll tell you exactly what I think," she said.

"I was born in 1956 in Brookfield, Wisconsin. It was easy for my parents. They were both working people, but as a middle-class family we could go out every Friday night if we wanted to for a fish fry. We never had to worry about how to pay our bills. We all had jobs with decent benefits. My mother was a nurse and my father was a salesman. My sisters and me all went to college. Our parents could pay for it. It just isn't like that anymore. I'm a recruiter that places engineers. But we don't know how we're going to make the payment if the car breaks down. I'm sixty and I'm done with it. I just can't do this anymore.

"I am a person of middle income and it has been very tough for my family. Manufacturing has been hit hard. A lot of jobs have left because China and Mexico can get away with emissions because they don't have regulations. I think free trade has been misrepresented. I'm disappointed. I want to see this country go back to what it used to be.

"The country is more racist than ever. I can speak from experience. I have a special-needs son and I have minority people in my house every day. Have for eleven years. I go to work, and they help me take care of my son. The problem is, they're working three or four jobs. And if they earn 'X' amount of dollars, they lose every benefit they have. I think that that's something that needs to be looked at. These are hard-working women. The fathers are not in the homes. They want to earn a decent income but the policies say, if you earn $20,000 or $25,000, you're going to be completely cut off from food stamps if you need them, heating assistance if you need it, daycare assistance if you need it."

I tell her she sounds like a bleeding heart liberal.

"It's not liberal. It's smart and moderate. These women want to work and earn a decent income, but the policies and their communities are holding them back. I'm a conservative and have been a Republican all of my life. I'm tired of the Republican Party telling me they'll do something about the budget or immigration and not get it done. Everyone has to balance their budgets and they need to as well. We have to protect our borders and not let illegal immigrants come in and get benefits that legal immigrants can't have. Trump can get it done. He is so great at listening and brings in so many brilliant people around him."

As Kathy spoke, a thirty-something Milwaukee man named John Lusz lurked nearby, murmuring an occasional dissent. When I asked him what he cared about, he said, "Muslims and Mexicans." But his resentment of undocumented migrants didn't stop him from employing them in his small packaging business.

"I'm guilty," he said. "I employ illegals. Pay them cash. It's tough when it's there. I feel very guilty about it. It's just wrong. They don't pay in, but they want the stuff. Collecting social services, with a cash-hustle on the side. They should learn English. I won't go anywhere that has bilingual signs. Don't mind Braille. Braille is fine."

The line started to move. At the entrance, I found myself behind an enormous fellow in a camo jacket explaining to security, "I have rods in my body. That's why the alarm is gonna go off."

The man's name was Danny Kapalczynski. I knew all about the metal rods in his body because we'd both arrived at the rally early and spent a couple of hours together in the high school parking lot. Like Anthony Holston in Phoenix, Kapalczynski depended on social services to get him through, a mix of veterans' benefits and Medicaid. He wasn't proud of this, but he wasn't ashamed, either, even if he preferred to call Medicaid by its local euphemism, BadgerCare. A native of West Allis, Kapalczynski remembered the smell of industry that defined the community he grew up in during the 1970s. He said he was hopeful Trump could bring back some smokestacks, and maybe sprinkle a few nuclear bombs over the Middle East.

"The name Kapalczynski is Polish-German. Jewish, actually. My mother is a full-blooded Jew. We moved to Wisconsin after my dad got out of the military in '73. I was four years old. I graduated from Eisenhower High School in New Berlin, Waukesha County, just outside Milwaukee. After school, I moved to West Allis, because I couldn't afford nothing in New Berlin.

"I've been in politics since I was ten. My first campaign, my dad's buddy was running for alderman in New Berlin. I helped stuff mailboxes. Waking up at five in the morning, rolling flyers in rubber bands, putting them in the newspaper box. Stan Smith—thank God he won. The alderman in his district, you'd call the office and never get hold of him. The neighborhood lawns would have seven or eight beat-up cars in the front yard. Nobody ever did nothing about it. Nothing would ever get fixed. The local politicians, the aldermen, they're still lining their pockets. Maybe they work one or two days a week. If you're lucky, you can catch them on a Wednesday. Thursday and Friday they're all out golfing together. I'd love to go on seven vacations a year. Maybe I should run for office. I should spend six months a year golfing with my buddies, watching the sunrise somewhere down in the Bahamas. That would be great. Never have done it. Been working. I've been a machinist and automotive-finish painter most of my life. I've also built homes. Different kinds of seasonal work.

"When I was growing up, the economy was good. We had Pelton Steel. Got the ore from Iron Mountain, Michigan. All the big iron industries were here. We had foundries. We had machining companies. It was all done right here. Now it's all done overseas. My dad worked in the foundries and was a foundry teacher at Milwaukee Area Technical College, the downtown campus. When he retired fifteen years ago, he said it was because there were no apprenticeships anymore. Pelton Steel had closed. Everybody was downsizing. Now there are only two foundries left, Star in Waukesha, and Maynard's in Milwaukee. They can do the same job in China for $2.30 [an hour] that costs $28 here. That's what killed us. Now our biggest industry is shipping scrap metal. Nothing is made here. If you look at the small American flags, they're all made in China. We don't even make pencils. Pencils!

"I'm not a union breaker. I believe in the unions. They were good at the time. But today, if you're paying the American guy $20, and the guy in China will do it for $3, and shipping is free, what are you gonna do? You gotta figure out a happy medium. Everybody's gotta have a fair wage, gotta make a living. But it's not happening anymore. McDonald's isn't a stepping-stone job. It's a career. Because they can't find nothing else. When big industry does come, the job line looks like a food line.

"People here are working at Walmart, they're working at Kmart. They're working at a sub shop. McDonald's. Target. You go downtown, where Pelton and Nordberg and all [the manufacturing plants] used to be, it's parking lots. Here in West Allis, the old Allis-Chalmers factory was seven miles long, two miles wide. They used to make tractors and tractor parts, all sorts of stuff. They shut down in the '80s. Now it's a giant parking lot, there's a shoe store. I've been there when they close the doors. I was there in the late '90s when AutoTech pulled out of Waukesha. We built plating machines. I worked for $19 an hour. They moved to Brazil where they can build that equipment for four or six dollars a day.

"That's why so many people are here waiting hours [to hear Trump]. You could just go down this line and ask people: 'How many of your dads are still working? How many are unemployed? How many took early retirement just so they wouldn't lose their benefits? How many took early retirement, and *still* got screwed out of their benefits anyways?' Look at Pabst. Pabst Brewing Company. Right here in Milwaukee, one of the biggest breweries we had. Miller bought it and closed the shop. The employees who retired got screwed. The buildings were vacant for years. Now some of them are condos.

"It all happened so slowly the American people didn't see it going down. I've voted Democrat a couple of times. Ninety-eight percent of the time, I vote Republican, because they aren't politically correct. But I blame both parties equally. Everyone had hands in their pockets, greasing the wheel. 'Give me a couple million and I'll sign this into law.'

"To bring back big industry, you'd have to close the borders and say, 'Start making it here, or we're not having it here.'

Build the wall. My great-grandparents came here legally. They did the [immigration] paperwork. But jumping a fence and then getting free health care, free college—are you kidding me? I took on two jobs to help my son go to college. I didn't want him being in the same position I was. Now he's the head supervisor at Maynard's for shipping and receiving. He's already ahead of the game. That's what it's all about. The next generation doing a little better. But he's got more taxes coming out of his pocket to pay for all the bullshit. Free services for illegal immigrants? I had to fight six months to get food stamps after my back injury. Had to fight to get $126 a month because I'm not working. I'm from here, my whole life. I come from middle-class, working people, my whole life. And this is the way we get treated. It's gotta stop. I'm sick of people saying, 'Oh, you can't say this because they're black or they're Mexican.' It doesn't matter. We all bleed the same color of blood. I've learned this because my mom's Jewish. Ethnicity means nothing to me. [Trump's campaign] isn't about race. It's about people having enough. Putting their foot down and saying, 'Hey, this guy's speaking the truth.'

"My last job was making drive shafts for the big windmills. When everybody caught on that was a big scam, we started downsizing. They let eight of us go, out of thirty-two. That winter, I hurt my back shoveling ice. Three vertebrae. I lost two and a half inches. Now I can't lift anything over ten pounds. When it's nice out, I sit in the back yard with my dog. I watch the grass grow.

"The health care system sucks. I could barely afford it when my company was paying for half. Then it was out of my own pocket and I had to pay a $15,000 deductible. I had to hit *fifteen grand*, the cost of a nice used car, before they start paying anything out. Most of the hospitals that I went to wouldn't take Obamacare. Finally, my friend was like, 'Hey man, you're not making a dime, you've paid in your whole life, there's no reason you can't get on BadgerCare.' So I got on BadgerCare. It's Medicaid, basically. But it's BadgerCare. Now I pay $69 a year.

"Bernie Sanders wants universal health care for everybody. It's 'free,' right? What is 'free'? It means [someone's] going to be paying more because I'm hurt and can't work? Nothing is free. That's a sham. My dad taught me, when I was a little kid, if it's free, it's bullshit. Ain't nothing in this world free. Everybody pays taxes and dies. You might get it for free, but then there's five other people paying for it. Let's be real. That's why I like Trump. He's real.

"I believe in a nice minimum wage, maybe $10. But the more you go up, the more you're shooting yourself in your foot. Watch what happens in California. And Billy's making $15 at McDonald's, but G.I. Joe's only making $9? If you join the service right now, you're making $9.25 an hour. He's defending our country wearing a helmet and a gun, but Billy who never graduated high school is making $15 flipping a burger.

"I served in Kuwait during Operation Desert Storm. We shouldn't have been there. Same with Iraq in '03. Trump is right. Now Obama wants to close Guantanamo and put them on a plane and send them back so they can go kill more Americans. How stupid is that? Waterboard 'em to death. Make 'em talk. Eye for an eye. It's in the Bible. I say drop the [nuclear] bomb on ISIS. Scare the shit out of all of them, the countries around them. It'll stop. We haven't had this much trouble since Japan. We dropped the bombs on Japan and that shit all stopped, too. Let them cool off for 20, 30 years. I've lost friends over there. I have cousins that I worry about now every day. Why are we sending them into harm's way?

"They come back, and there's a wait-list at the VA. People are living in their cars outside the VA. And it's getting worse. Guys are coming back with PTSD. About twenty-seven a day are committing suicide. The military teaches you to kill, it doesn't teach you how to live with killing. Nobody wants to say, 'I'm at the lowest point in my life, and I need help.' Nobody wants to say that. And nobody's saying, 'Hey, buddy, you fought for us, lemme help you.' We're forgetting them. Trump doesn't.

"As soon as I get my disability settlement, I'm out of here. Like my dad. He lives in a cabin upstate. He's been up there almost 15 years. I got some land up there. I'm gonna put a trailer on it, or something cheap. If shit ever really does hit the fan, the city is the last place you wanna be. We got people who already don't give a shit. Imagine when the truckers aren't trucking food and the gasoline is gone. When the preppers [people who prepare for imminent collapse of civilization] first came out, people laughed at them. Now they're scratching their head, saying, 'Maybe they know something we don't.'

"My family up north grows their own food. My aunts and uncles take care of a three-and-a-half acre garden. My dad and my uncle split a cow every year. So, I'll be going in on that. It's cheaper. Buy half a cow and that meat will last you the whole year. It works out to around $1.89 a pound. There's tons of prepper communities up north now. They'll say 'Hi,' but they don't invite you over until you've been there awhile. That'll change once I get up there and they know I'm not just a 'shacker' from the city, just visiting for a weekend. Up north, everybody takes care of each other. When Joe the Neighbor's wife is in the hospital, you go over and feed his cows.

"If things don't change, something's gotta give. The people up north are getting ready. You can tell the prepper communities because they're fenced in. For years, you'd drive up there and just see a house, set back in the woods a little bit. Now, that house has a nine-foot barbed wire fence. Common sense."

* * *

A few days before the primary, I met up with Dennis Vlach, the realtor from Serb Hall, for breakfast at an A&M chain restaurant. Sitting in a corner booth, Vlach explained that the financial and real estate crises were caused by poor people and the Community Reinvestment Act, which helped many low-income earners buy homes. Vlach's animus toward Obama sounded oddly personal, and it soon became clear why. Vlach had gone through a nasty and expensive divorce during Obama's 2008 campaign and election. "Nothing was good enough for my ex-wife," he explained during one of several asides on the subject. He was still bitter about it. Vlach was bitter about a lot of things, which he explained over waffles and a dozen cups of weak Wisconsin diner coffee.

"My grandparents immigrated to Milwaukee from Czechoslovakia. My father was a welder, solder, and worked on five acres in the country town of Raymond, just south of here. He died the weekend before I started first grade. My mom was too proud to go on welfare. She worked as a janitor across the street and grew food. I was number five out of six: three sisters, two brothers. When I was eleven, I went with my mother to drop off my older brother at the cabbage farms. They grabbed me, too. You had to be twelve for a work permit, so they withheld my wages until my birthday. Farm labor paid less than a dishwasher. It was a dollar an hour. I saved up money. Brought food home. My mom kept most of my paychecks. After five years, I was foreman at the farm making $1.50 an hour, supervising kids older and younger than me. There was planting season, then you worked in the pulling patches. I also worked as a dishwasher and went to school. I've never been without a job since I was eleven years old. Ever.

"Back then in Racine County, Johnson's Wax was the number one industry. Cabbage production was number two. I remember, one day, our company sent out forty-two semi loads of cabbage. In one day. Some bigger shippers maybe sent out one hundred. That's a lot of cabbage. I learned early on pulling cabbage how stupid the media is. One picture in a paper showed me planting cabbage, with the caption, 'Picking cabbage.' Are you that stupid? My mother ended up being a reporter. She had seven years of education, up in Stetson. Her father didn't let her go to high school. Big family. She had to milk the cows.

"This was farm labor. What they can't get people to do today. Get up early, go in. It's dirty work. Hard work. I did not enjoy it. You come home, take a shower, darn near clog the drain, but you're tired. Just went to bed. You didn't have the aggravation of knowing that, say, *Obama* is president and screwing up our country terribly. Even Jimmy Carter is a distant second as terrible.

"I was in college at UW-Milwaukee when Carter was there. It was tough. I was pumping gas and changing tires. My brother had a machine shop making valve stems. OSHA closed him down for not using the proper cutting fluids, and so forth, fluids that were, let's say, better. Government regulation. I also worked in hotel security at the Red Carpet Hotel. I remember Ted Kennedy was there when I applied. It would have been 1980. When I left in 1985, I was already working as a realtor. I made Salesman of the Year while working at the hotel full-time. So you see my work ethic, compared to

Bernie Sanders and the party of 'Give me free stuff'? Risk, reward. Democrats don't understand that free is not free.

"I'm meeting a man later this afternoon, a very wealthy gentleman, who owns a lot of rentals. He worked and saved. He has that bumper sticker of Calvin peeing on Obama. He's sick of the corruption, the taxation. These are the people that keep the economy going. He's for Trump. Talking to people I know, I'd say two-thirds of small businessmen around here are supporting Trump. We need a businessman, not more unions.

"The UAW [United Auto Workers] screwed things up around here, royal. We used to have American Motors in Kenosha. We used to have Allis-Chalmers in West Allis, a big international company. They made the turbines for the Hoover Dam. Too much unions, too much government. High taxes. Now they're replaced by Kmart, things like that. Now the average person living on entitlements is better off than the average person working. That can't be. Who's gonna pay for it? Bernie Sanders? He's a deadbeat. He didn't get his first job until he was forty. He thinks big business is evil. But we need them to prosper. If we tax them too much, they hide their money instead of reinvesting it here. Trump is the only one who'll crack down on that. Only he can do that. That's what separates him from Cruz and Kasich. Any normal American president can handle ISIS. Only Trump understands business. Anybody who's worth over $10 billion is a smart guy."

I ask Vlach about Milwaukee's foreclosure crisis and his own rental business.

"Being a landlord—there are clogged toilets, broken heaters. People don't understand. I currently have over $100,000 in judgments against tenants. I'll never get it. It's worthless paper. I have this attorney, he's a retired judge, right down the street here, he does my evictions. He enjoys evicting these tenants. It's what he does in his pastime. That's probably a good attorney to have. The judges are part of the good-old-boy network. They know what they're doing."

After a mental double-take, I realize that Vlach is using "the good-old-boy network" in a positive sense. For him, Trump resonates with a yearning for when the "good-old-boy network" was national and taken for granted—providing a kind of club-member-level protection known today as privilege and supremacy. Maintaining these networks, even at the municipal level, is harder than it used to be. But Vlach is no doubt correct in suggesting they thrive still in Milwaukee. Like he said, these judges know what they're doing.

Chapter Three

Pennsylvania

I was pulling into the crowded parking lot of the Harrisburg Farm Show Expo Center when the Corolla rolled into earshot. Out of its open windows thundered a song at full volume, straining the speakers to the edge of noise mud. There was no mistaking the tune. The hook broke through all the shaking, boomy bass like a star-spangled monster truck breaks through a wall of fire doing a wheelie. Before I could rummage up the song's name, its lyrics commanded that I scream along—"*FUCK YEAH!*"—or be raghead-commie-pussy road stain.

I know this song, "America (Fuck Yeah)," the way most people do, as satire, as the steroidal-jingoist theme song to *Team America*, Trey Parker and Matt Stone's puppet-performed 2004 war-on-terror spoof. Not that long ago, I would have marveled at the sight of kids in American flag gear blasting it as a pump-up party song. But this is a year when not that long ago can feel like a long time ago. At a rally to make America great again, in the middle of Pennsylvania, the song made perfect sense. What else *but* "America (Fuck Yeah)" could be the unofficial anthem of Trump tailgating? Why didn't the campaign have it blaring *inside* the rallies, instead of that unsettling mix featuring movie-mob-restaurant Puccini and white-boy party rap like House of Pain's "Jump Around"? On second thought, maybe Trump's rally music is already a pretty good fit.

I exchanged devil's horns with the five college-aged guys in the Corolla, who were passing around what looked like a plastic bottle filled with cranberry and vodka. I did my best to sing the words I knew:

America, FUCK YEAH!
McDonalds, FUCK YEAH!
Walmart, FUCK YEAH!
NFL, FUCK YEAH!
Rock and roll, FUCK YEAH!
The Internet, FUCK YEAH!
Slavery, FUCK YEAH!

Slavery? I'd never noticed that in the lyrics before. Maybe this millennial conservative appropriation was more layered than it looked, involving levels of irony I was born a little too late to appreciate. Or maybe there was no self-awareness happening at all, and I was witnessing the truth of the old state saw that Pennsylvania is Philadelphia and Pittsburgh with Alabama in the middle. I took a good look at the kids, who by now were alongside me. Drunkenly screaming "Fuck Yeah!" in Trump hats and American flag shirts, they looked earnest and knew all the words by heart. They were probably five years old when *Team America* came out during the 2004 presidential campaign. Had they even seen the movie?

After parking, I found them standing around the beer-filled trunk of their Corolla. They took turns shotgunning cans of Coors Light, whooping each other on and filming every chug for posting on Snapchat. I introduced myself and they passed me the bottle of cranberry and vodka. They were fraternity brothers at a local Christian college, but declined to name it. I was with a cameraman, and they suspected I was a mole from a local chapter of campus Democrats. "Wait a second," said a kid in an Abbie Hoffman–style American flag shirt, "this is like one of those videos on Facebook where you attack us." But they were wasted, and couldn't resist the camera. The drunkest and most belligerent of the bunch stepped up in sunglasses and said, "Bernie Sanders—not a fan. Fuck that community college bullshit. Trump all the way, dude. We're gonna build that wall, we're gonna take the immigrants out of our country. That's what we're gonna do. That's what the rally's *about*, baby."

More of their friends arrived, more beers were crushed to "America (Fuck Yeah)", and they left as a pack to join the thousands-strong rally line, holding aloft an oversized Trump flag like Brazilians at the World Cup. They were gone before I could ask them if they'd ever seen *Team America*.

The line outside the Harrisburg Farm Show Center was enormous even by the sold-out standards of Trump campaign events. It looped around the entire lot and back into itself, forming a kind of messy seashell spiral. Thousands chose to stay in line even after word rippled through that Trump was already speaking, and it was obvious they wouldn't make it to the door in time. Those who did make it to the entrance found a police line around a few dozen protestors chanting "Black Lives Matter!" at attendees who responded, "Blue Lives Matter!" Meanwhile, on stage, Trump struggled to express the concept of altruism without him at the center, still "taking" things. After a lifetime of "taking"—"That's what I do, I take, I take, I take"—he promised to "take for you, the country."

The Trump parking-lot scene is different from the others. At its liveliest, it is part NFL, part political circus. The Harrisburg lot was thick with vendors selling everything but Trump-branded cotton candy. The most popular item, sold by several members of a local black family, was a T-shirt with "Hillary Sucks, but not like Monica!" on the front, and "Trump That Bitch!" on the back. Then there are the characters, guys like Mark Spence whom I met in Wisconsin, who joyfully bounce around in face paint reciting the gospel of Paul Harvey.

Then there are the boozers. They're usually middle-aged men with bodies that no longer respond well to standing in long lines. So they show their support at rallies by drinking with friends, pouring cups for strangers, cheering on the crowd, maybe scaring away a reporter or two. This was pretty much the exact profile of Jay Brandt, the fifty-four-year-old construction contractor who held court over the loudest tailgate in Harrisburg. I heard his laugh from 100 yards away, and followed it until I found a goateed bear of a man in a camo Trump cap sitting on the back of a shiny black Ford pickup. As I walked up, he was wiping a splash of vodka and Sprite from his crisp denim Carhart overalls. Next to Brandt cackled a much smaller man, Ben Calhoun, his best buddy from childhood and obviously the submissive sidekick in the friendship. "Make me another drink," said Brandt, handing his friend a plastic cup emblazoned with a bald eagle.

They gave me a drink and we chatted about the line. When I told Brandt I was a reporter, he tilted his head back and pointed at me. "Are you for *real*? Look in my eyes. Are you a bomber? You need a shave. Are you a bomber? Are you with Hillary?" The inquisition made Calhoun double over in laughter. When he recovered, he said, "This chick from NPR came by, like, two hours ago. She said, 'Can I interview you?' And we were, like, "Uh, *no*. You're from NPR!""

A third man who'd been listening in, said, "How many people tailgate at a *political rally*? Only Trump—this is a whole different campaign." This was Ron Tamecki, a sales manager for a bow company who'd come to the rally alone and gravitated to Brandt's truck.

I agreed the Trump campaign was different. I explained that that was the reason I was traveling the country talking to its supporters. I asked Brandt about the central Pennsylvania he grew up in, how it's changed, and how Trump might make the country great again. He asked me again if I was "for real," and told me to put my recorder down on the truck bed and let it roll.

"I was born and raised in Mechanicsburg. That's fifteen miles from here, on the other side of the river. My family all came into the port of Philadelphia in the 1700s. There was no Ellis Island. We weren't immigrants. We were *settlers*. Germans like us all moved to Central Pennsylvania. For generations, we were orchard farmers. This was farming country. It's suburban now. I left. Now I live out towards Shippensburg in the middle of fifty-two acres of woodland.

"I've known this guy since sixth grade—I'd be a veterinarian right now if it wouldn't be for that fucking jackass," he said, jerking a thumb at Calhoun, who cracked up. "The Pennsylvania we grew up in, in Mechanicsburg, it was lily white. The only time we had color in our school was during apple picking season. The kids of the black folks would be in our school. They were traveling migrant workers, here 'cause of the apple industry in Adams and Cumberland Counties. You had two or three, and they'd *vamos* after picking season. Our senior year, a black fella came into our class and started dating an upper-class white girl. In those days, you'd be ashamed to have an interracial child. But we didn't say anything. We are not hateful. We didn't give a shit. We're white crackers, but we're not prejudiced. This campaign is not a race thing.

"In the late '70s, man, we lived life. We used to get these Colombian ounces of weed, four fingers deep, thirty-five bucks. We'd roll bones, have a great fuckin' time. I can't smoke the new shit. It knocks your dick up into your shirt pocket. After school, we'd go shoot groundhogs, possums, shoot doves. At school, we all had guns in our trucks, guns in our cars. Try that *now*. It's a 'gun-free zone.' Everything is becoming so fucking soft. Trump is a first step to getting back to that old school thinking.

Calhoun pretended to cower in fear at the mention of guns: "Help! I need a safe space!"

Brandt screamed for help. "Ben needs a safe space!"

The friends laughed for a long minute before Brandt got back to his story.

"I started working in construction at thirteen. My old man was a drywall contractor. I worked on stilts, sanding drywall, stocking drywall, cleaning drywall. It paid for school. I went to Temple University, class of '85. Got a degree in finance and business management. I would have been a '84 graduate, however—you see these holes in my head?" He pointed to his temples. "They're from two big screws I had in the sides of my head after Jimmy Carter broke my motherfuckin' neck."

I bit. "How did Jimmy Carter break your neck?"

"In 1980, interest rates were—" he stopped to observe me. "I don't know how old you are, fella."

I told him forty-one, but he didn't believe me. I handed him my driver's license and he shared it with Calhoun, whispering, "Ben, I can't even read his last name. I think this guy's a Unabomber."

The men laughed, causing Brandt to spill his drink again. He sent Calhoun to the front of the truck to fix him another.

"So this is how Carter broke my neck. After my first year at Temple in '81, interest rates were like twenty-two percent. For the first time, my father had no work for me. So my mother got me a job with Miller & Norford Construction, carrying cement, pans, tying steel. I was a frickin' mule. It was an hour-and-a-half commute to the site. One day during the ride, a '75 Thunderbird rear-ended my foreman's '73 VW Bug. Broke my neck. A hangman's fracture. It's all fused together now, my C2 and C3. If that son of a bitch Carter wouldn't have run the goddamned country into the shitter, my old man would have been home building, and we would have had work. That's how Jimmy Carter broke my fuckin' neck. My folks were Democrats. Back then, that's what working folk were. When I turned eighteen in 1980, my first election, I voted for Ronald Wilson Reagan.

"When I was at Temple, I was a teamster. I worked evenings and weekends for United Parcel Service. After the graveyard shift, we'd shave and go to class, all huffed up on fuckin' meth. For holiday season, they wanted you to do a double shift. I would go right from working doubles to [Temple's suburban] Ambler Campus, all pumped up on frickin' meth. I'd have these 300-level classes like operations management, with lots of statistics. I'd meth up and go to the library. Nobody would see me for days. They called me 'Rosie' because I could fall in a pile of shit and come up smelling like a rose.

"I became a contractor in 1999. Now people work for me. My dad was against it. He told me the human element would destroy me, and he was right. I pass his grave every single day, and every time I say, 'Dad, you were right.' Undocumented workers aren't really an issue in Pennsylvania. Once I did hire a Mexican crew. They piled out of a Dodge Dakota like it was a clown car. They all had green cards. I registered them, did all that shit. The first job they did fuckin' great. The next job was tough, a tear-off job, and two days into it, they fuckin' *vamos*'d. I'm ashamed to say it, but I deal with white boys on drugs, and drunken white boys. My best crew is a great crew, but they have demons. I mean, who's being a roofer? You want to be a roofer? It's tough work. Nobody wants to do it. A lot of the guys do heroin. They snort it. I don't know what the fuck they do with it."

I asked Brandt about Trump's plans to tear up trade deals and slap tariffs on U.S. companies that move factories abroad. He said, "The American worker has gotten a raw deal, like Trump says. We're selling ourselves down the river with these trade agreements."

Tamecki, the third wheel, exclaimed, "Bethlehem Steel! My God, it's gone. It's ArcelorMittal [an Indian-owned multinational steel company headquartered in Luxembourg] now. It's barely there."

"It's not just steel," added Calhoun. "Textiles. Gone. They went down south. Then they went further south. People do whatever's left. A lot of service industry, some warehousing jobs. Amazon has a distribution center close by. If you make $12.50 an hour, you're lucky. I'll tell you a story. In 1981, when I was in college, I worked as a casual dockworker, a teamster job. I made $13.13 an hour. My mom knew the terminal manager. I could call him up and get two-day weekend shifts. You know, favored. I went back there five years ago. You know what they started me at? *Ten-fifty*. Thirty 'effin years later! It's bullshit."

Temecki, who grew up in a mining community, described the fate of the old coal towns: "All my family worked the mines. When I was a kid, I used to go and help pick coal. You'd go in at dark, come out at dark, go to the bar, clean your lungs out with some beers and whiskey, go to sleep for a couple hours, get up, and do it again. Everything was black. Your shirt right there, black. You're whole house was black, your hands were black, your nails were black, your eyes would be just . . . ." He trailed off.

"The towns are still there. They're tight towns. You have Polacks, Slovaks, Italians. Everyone still lives in a little town-house, 'half a double,' it was called. If you did good or moved up in the mines, you could buy the other half, and you'd have a whole house. All those people never recovered. It's all gone now. The jobs. The smart ones escaped. Lots of welfare, welfare, welfare.

"There's lots of Trump support in these towns. They are just tired of everything. I promise you, it's a fifty- or sixty-year-old guy who's seen everything, like us. And he's, like, 'We don't see change. We don't see it. We tried. We voted Democrat. We voted Tea Party.' Nothing's working. Maybe they were Ross Perot voters, and now, it's like, 'Here is our last chance. If we don't do it now, we're going to go to our grave and it's never going to happen.' That's what I think is driving this. It is the last chance."

* * *

From Harrisburg, I drove east, to Greene and Fayette Counties, the twin capitals of Pennsylvania coal. Until the last few elections, the area was a reliable Democratic strong-hold, where most breadwinners held United Mine Workers union cards. But the old allegiances have been weakening in recent cycles with the local economy. There were reports of fifth-generation Democrats switching parties to vote for

Trump. A once-thriving regional economy had been hollowed out to what Jim Davis, the Democratic Party chairman of Fayette County, described in a radio interview as "a landscape of little towns in different levels of decay."

Driving south from Pittsburgh, it didn't take long to start hitting these towns in decay. On a gray and drizzly afternoon, much of Clairton, population seven thousand, resembled the abandoned industrial town at the beginning of Tarkovsky's *Stalker*. The main drag is a museum of shuttered businesses under faded signs from another age. The window of the town's gas station mini-mart is covered with "Wanted" stills from the surveillance camera, with nicknames scrawled beneath blurry images of petty criminals: "cheese danish thief," "medicine thief," "5 hour energy thief," "hamburger thief," "dumbest candy thief." And Clairton is one of the luckier towns, where the old industry survives in the scaled-down production of the local coke plant, still the country's biggest, whose belching skyline of piping and smokestacks still produces the forgotten sibling in the triad of coal-coke-steel.

The coal trains still arrive in Clairton from places like Carmichaels, Greene County, one of the state's better-known coal towns. For a century, coal defined most aspects of life in places like Carmichaels. Politics tracked with the union, which grew strong under the forty-year reign of New Dealer John L. Lewis. The King Coal Association, meanwhile, has for the better part of a century thrown the biggest social event of the calendar, an annual Coal Festival presided over by a local teenage beauty anointed Coal Queen.

I parked in Carmichaels on a Saturday afternoon and walked through the center of town. Though more bucolic than Clairton, it felt as empty. I followed a street past the sole stoplight until I came to a sign announcing Pappy's Lounge. Inside, a handful of people sat around the windowless bar. The female bartender, a forty-something firecracker with auburn hair, sized me up and told me I was welcome at Pappy's. She said, "Some bars here don't like outsiders coming in. I like it. You hear interesting stories." When I said I was a reporter here for the election, she laughed, "Oh, no. We don't talk religion or politics here. It never ends well."

What people did talk about around the bar at Pappy's was sex, gossip, and mining. A retired miner at the bar toasted me as I hoisted a bottle of Yuengling, Pennsylvania's finest, and offered to get me up to speed.

"Around here, you got gas wells and you got coal mines," he said. "More than a third work in the mines. I've watched it all go to hell. Bob Murray [the coal magnate and CEO of Murray Energy]—he don't give a shit about the workers. It's, 'Wink wink, get the coal out and be safe. I ain't paying you shit, though.' He owns mines here, some in Utah. He's trying to break the union. When the contracts come up, he won't budge. He shuts down the mines for one year and a day. Then he opens them back up with nonunion labor at lower pay. He just hires all new workers. Jobs down in the mine used to be $35 or $38 an hour, now it's $25. The union used to be strong, but not anymore."

A younger, heavier man in a backward Browns cap chimed in from the other end of the bar. "You know who you should talk to, is my roommate, Stanley," he said. "He's an old-timer. Used to vote Democrat, now he's with Trump. I am, too. Big time. He's having his chemo today, but maybe we can all meet tomorrow."

The following morning, I visited John Beatty and his roommate Stanley Stockdale at their trailer home located high in the green hills outside Carmichaels. The air smelled of stale cigarettes, the walls were decorated with paintings of Indians. A dozen porcelain eagles crowded a cabinet next to a wide-screen television. The men were a bit of an Odd Couple: Stockdale, sixty-nine, taciturn, wiry, and neat in a button down tucked into his jeans. Beatty, twenty years younger, chatty, fat, a loose Cleveland Browns jersey hanging off his frame, which was still massive after losing a hundred pounds following a heart attack. Stockdale, though trim, is no healthier. He wheezes from thirty-three years in the mines, and has stage-four cancer of the lungs and brain.

Beatty has a palpable admiration and love for his dying friend. When I'd met him at Pappy's, he gushed like a proud son that Stockdale knew as much about mining as anyone in the county. "When Stanley started," he said, "they still used canaries to test the oxygen. They chose canaries because they have such a tiny lung capacity. If they dropped over, it meant methane was eating up the oxygen. It meant get out of there, quick."

Beatty looked on with pride the next afternoon, as Stockdale talked about trucking and mining, and the switch from voting Democrat to voting Trump.

"My family is from right here, a long ways back. They were farmers, all the way up and down the ladder. I was the youngest of seven. Growing up, it was a situation where you did what you had to do, and you busted your ass doing it. I started working in the womb. We had a little dairy farm, grew our own beef. It was milking cows, work the hay, more hay. A whole bunch of hay [laughs]. I was usually up and on the roll about six in the morning. That was year round. I didn't like farm work.

"In the '60s, I moved to Detroit and got married. Drove trucks, long-haul semis, for ten years. Driving trucks is tough on a marriage, but the major problem was the bitch couldn't keep her panties on. We divorced. I came back here, filled out an application for the mines. Got hired by Consol. Back then they were all union jobs. I bought this place in the early '70s. The land is mine clear down to the wood line.

"Miners worked swing shifts back then. One week, you'd be on days, the next week afternoons, the third week, you'd be on graveyard. That's how it worked. It was rough. You wouldn't any more get used to this shift than you were onto the next shift. You had trouble adapting, especially coming off midnights, even if it was always dark down there anyway. I never knew why they did it that way, but that's the way they did it. After a certain amount of time, you could bid for jobs that were steady shift.

"We'd follow the machines and bolt the roof and put the coal in the scoops, ten feet at a time. Once an area was drilled out, you moved to the next one—cut, dig, bolt—then went right back to the first one and started all over again. Ten more feet. That's not even safe, ten feet, but it's safer than going further than ten feet. I got covered up in coal twice. The worse one, I was bolting the roof in an area that had a loose top. We'd bolt only every four feet. I went to drill a hole and when I sank the bit, the top splintered and a big chunk come down on me. That's when I screwed up my back, my leg, my neck. I was out of work about six weeks. Not long enough. I was still in pain. But the company, it was, like, 'When are you coming back to work?'"

John interrupted, saying, "And that was in a union mine. Now there are union and nonunion mines. My nephew works for a Bailey mine, which is nonunion. He makes big money hourly, but the benefits suck. That's why everybody wants to be union. He got a four-dollar pay cut, and is only working four days a week. It's either that, or you have no job. Years ago, there was a steady medium."

Stanley shook his head in agreement. He continued: "Years ago, you went to work at eight o'clock in the morning and you worked until four o'clock that afternoon, and you come home, and went back to the same situation. And every ten days you swung shifts. There's no comparison to what there was then. I got out in 2010 making a union rate, $60-plus an hour. But a lot of guys are still working, trying to make that, and there's no way they're going to. At Bailey, they're working four days a week, if they're lucky, making $25 or $30 an hour. In my situation, I'm retired. I have my pension, and I have my Social Security. I'm basically set. But what about all these other people struggling?

"I'm originally a Democrat, but they've changed so drastically. They don't support solid fuels. That's why the coal mines are shutting down. There's no market there for the coal, so, shut it down. And it just keeps going on and on and getting deeper and deeper. A lot of coal miners went elsewhere. We've had several coal mines close down. Not just one or two. This economy went from being . . . lower middle class, to being basically a depressed area. The coal industry in this area meant absolutely everything. Probably seventy-five percent of this area had an affiliation with the coal industry."

Beatty cut in again: "I've heard the term 'dumb coal miner' many times in my life. Each time, it agitates me. We're the little men, understand, we live in this little community, we're rural, we're out in the woods, we're not to be heard. We don't have a voice, okay? Well, we do. I'm tired of watching my friends and family suffer, listening to the Democrats make coal the enemy. I'm telling you, it's all Obama's doing. Until he took office, coal around here was thriving. My whole family was involved with the coal industry. My uncle was boss in a mine. His wife worked as a secretary. Both their kids got out of high school and went right into mining. And then you look at Obama on television—you know what I am saying? When you have no concerns about your fellow man. . . . This is why I never talk about this kind of stuff when I'm drinking.

Because it agitates the hell out of me. If Obama cared a bit, he would look at this area. Pennsylvania, West Virginia, Indiana, even parts of Ohio. It's gone. Probably never will come back. I really believe that Donald Trump is the answer. Never in my lifetime have I felt like this about a candidate. I believe he gets into office and says, 'Okay, now let's start thinking about the little guy. All you politicians have your pockets padded, let's worry about the little man. . . .'

"I love Donald Trump's thoughts on a lot of different things. I'm not a bigot, but I like the idea of sealing our borders. I'm tired of calling somewhere and I'm talking to Mohammad Mohaqa, who has no idea, who sounds like he has a mouth full of marbles, and my cousin is out of work. That doesn't make sense to me. We're Americans. I understand that we live in a democracy. I'm a very educated man. I'm of above-average intelligence. But like I said, my cousin's out of work. He's got a wife and three kids he can't feed right now. They are on welfare, getting food stamps. He's worked his whole life. It makes no sense. America first. Punish companies moving the jobs.

"In the beginning, I thought, 'Trump, this guy is an asshole.' He's arrogant and crass, I'll give you that. Women don't like him much, other than the ones that sleep with him. I won't call him a bigot, but he's not too far from it. But I believe the way that he thinks can do what has to be done. People think, 'Okay, this is enough of my son not having a job because Mohammad has one. That's enough of that.' I'm not against any foreign people, other than terrorists, obviously. But this is America. We have veterans on our streets. When you have a war veteran sleeping on cardboard, somebody dropped the ball. I don't believe Trump will allow that to happen any more, I really don't. I believe if he takes office, the economy is going to change. My biggest and only concern with him is he may create World War III.

"Instead of jobs around here, you got a lot of drugs. Used to be, people smoked some weed. We never got the crack epidemic like in Cleveland. Since this economy hit bottom, there's dope heads, heroin. Shooting it. People taking Xanny bars. One of my buddies found his kid with a needle hanging out of his arm, dead. From Fayette County all the way to Washington County. It would help if the coal mines started reopening and people could get jobs again, instead of loitering and sitting around. It becomes boring to anybody. A lot of people depend on that type of motivation. You know, 'Oh, man. I'm making $30 an hour. Let me get up and go to work.' I think the community would go back to the right path it was on, when we were in the coal mine.

"A mine is like a big family. Coal miners care about each other. Everybody loves everybody. I make homemade meatloaf that he loves still to this day." He smiled and shook a finger at Stanley. "I used to give it to him to make a couple sandwiches to put in his bucket, to take to the mine. Look, he's laughing already!" Both men broke out laughing. "Before lunchtime, he'd put his bucket on the charging station while he was out doing his thing. And everybody would be like, 'Sniff, sniff, what is that going on down there?' And he'd say, 'Get away from my lunch!' Those charging stations get really warm, like a stove. They'll heat your lunch. If you get cold down there, and you can get around one of them and work for a couple hours, life is good."

* * *

On the way back to Pittsburgh, I stopped in at the oldest miner's bar in Carmichaels, Serb's Red Star. The Serbian immigrant who opened the place in 1965, known affectionately as

"Serb," still tends bar most days and keeps up traditions that make the Red Star the Old McSorley's of Greene County—a quieter, all-male alternative to the coed, raunchy badinage at Pappy's, whose bartender described Serb's as "where the old codgers get together and hang out." Specifically, old codgers who vote Democrat. Serb runs a Democratic bar and still does. If there were a groundswell of Democratic support for Trump, he'd know.

But Serb wasn't in. "Out of town with his wife for a wedding," said the bartender, "Tiggie" Teegarden, a bearded, fit, and gruff middle-aged man in a Harley-Davidson shirt and a Pirates cap. "It's a shame you missed him," he said, cracking me a Yuengling. At the bar, a few men sullenly nursed beers and whiskeys. In one corner, someone played an old electronic poker game; in another, a tribe of plains Indians galloped across a muted TV tuned to the Western Channel. Above the bar hung a yellowed campaign poster for Bill DeWeese, a longtime regular and ex-House Speaker whose career in Pennsylvania politics ended on a raft of indictments for conflict of interest, theft, and criminal conspiracy. Or, as Tiggie put it with a shrug, "No worse than anybody else done."

I asked if any of Serb's regulars talked about voting for Trump.

"Not in here, they know better," he said. "But in Greene County, sure, there's been a lot of Dems switching for Trump, and some the other way around. A lot of party switching. I know a few of them. I'm not tempted. Trump wants to talk trade. He's blowing smoke. He just wants to badmouth everyone. It's pretty bad when the Pope comes out and says he doesn't like you. That's pretty bad.

"No [Democratic leaders] are for coal, though. They don't wanna touch it. The EPA comes up with all these goofy rules. They want to shut down all the power plants. Now, the big companies, like Alfa Natural Resources, what I work for, and Patriot, and Berch, they all want to take away the pension plans we were promised. Where will this place be? Alfa wants to take our vacation. Cut wages by six dollars. Do away with health and pensions. They want to hire contractors. It's all about profit. They're filing for bankruptcy. Well, who did that? Them guys did, the bosses. The workers did their jobs. We put the coal in the trains. I've worked for Alfa 37 years. Finished high school, then into the mines."

Teegarden went over to an old refrigerator in a small room behind the bar and brought back a jar. On a paper plate, he dumped out a pile of pickled cucumbers and onions slathered in balsamic vinegar. "The recipe called for normal oil, but these are pretty good," he said, handing me a fork.

He continued, "The natural gas boom is gone. We had gas rigs all over the place. All these people that made money off gas moved on. They shut 'em down when the price went down. All the gas companies that was here—very few people from Greene County got jobs. Halliburton brought Mexicans in from Texas, Oklahoma. You might have got a security guard job. Some of them hired a couple people. But they didn't train 'em. There was no proper safety. One local boy, a star athlete at the high school, a running back, got his head taken off. Rocky Doman. He was working on a well, just got outta high school. Another boy got killed on out toward Mount Morris. The explosion blew up everything around it. They could barely find the boy. That's how bad it was. The company wouldn't even let the DEP [Pennsylvania's Department of Environmental Protection] come in. It was four days before they let the federal government in. They don't want gas unionized like coal is.

"People out that way [in D.C., in New York] think we're dirtying the economy. That *is* our economy. Without the coal mines, we don't have no economy. They're closing stores left and right. They just closed the Kmart and the Sears in Uniontown. The only thing helping is gas prices are down. People can afford to drive out of county to work. If prices go up, they're gonna stay right here. All you're gonna have is ghost towns. Already do. Nimocal used to boom. Rice's Landing used to boom. Kids here, they don't work. Nothing here for 'em. They're going into the military. Or they're on dope. There's drugs, big time. Heroin overdoses. Crack. Started eight to ten years ago. In West Virginia, it's even worse."

West Virginia is where I was headed. I asked Teegarden if there's a town in the nearby Mountain State he'd recommend for talking coal and Trump. A man at the bar murmured, "All of 'em." He was right. The state's central coal counties had for months polled the highest levels of Trump support in the country, reflective of the candidate's promise to start "winning again" with coal. His "dig, baby, dig" mantra marked a sharp reversal for Trump, even by the "nothing matters" standards of his campaign. In December 2009, Trump signed a letter urging President Obama to take bold climate action "to avoid catastrophic and irreversible consequences for humanity and our planet." In April 2016, the idea that he ever cared about climate change was as fantastical as the new golden age he was promising the people of Appalachia.

Chapter Four

West Virginia

Along the wooded serpentine path of Coal River Road, it's common to see hunched figures emerge onto the two-lane blacktop, all dirtied up and shouldering what look like laundry bags. If the sacks are bulging, it was a good day up on the forested ridges digging up wild ginseng—or *sangin'* as they say in Raleigh County. The hills of southern West Virginia are rich with cash roots and ramps, of which ginseng is the most coveted on the global market. Once upon a pre-industrial time, sang, not coal, was king. Long before West Virginia statehood, the region sent wagon caravans of ginseng over the Federal Road to the spice capital of Baltimore, where it set sail for San Francisco and China. The first deposits of anthracite coal were unearthed in the same mountains, soon followed by some of the country's first coal mines. But China never stopped buying the local ginseng, or the paws and gallbladders of its black bears. When the mines opened, scavenging persisted as a rare alternative to picking coal. "Diggin's a rough life, and you gotta live poor," one harvester told me on Coal River Road. "But some always figured it's better than the mines."

Since the mines started closing, competition for ginseng has intensified in West Virginia's poorest counties. The state now regulates a four-month season to prevent overharvesting that threatens the root's extinction in the same mountains where automation and mountaintop blast mining have already transformed the old coal economy. Even those families that still have mining jobs sometimes supplement their declining incomes by sangin'. As in eastern Pennsylvania, many of West Virginia's new-century mining jobs are non-union and part-time, without the benefits or security of the jobs they replaced.

A spiral of poverty and depopulation has created quasi–ghost towns throughout the state's verdant hollows. The typical town is a modest church surrounded by the faded husks of social and commercial life: boarded-up shops, abandoned bowling alleys, the charred foundations of the last bar, burned down for the insurance payout. A sixty-one-year-old man from the hamlet of Coal Creek told me in bitter resignation, "We have a higher rate of refugees than Afghanistan and Syria. The whole valley is being depopulated. We lost our last grocery. The hardware store. Things that make a community."

Much of America is suffering hard times, but in deepest Appalachia, times have always been harder, even when times were good. When a January poll showed Trump's strongest support in the counties of southern West Virginia, it seemed to offer the explanatory power so many craved. West Virginia was poor, poorly educated, overwhelmingly white, in economic free fall. A rare beam of national media settled onto the state whose Facebook feeds burst with "help is on the way" Trump memes. A state that, like Trump, seemed a caricature of itself, a toothless monster of working-class anger, despair, alienation, bitterness, and defiance. Glossy magazines sent feature writers to Charleston. National newspapers published interactive maps promising, "How West Virginia Explains Donald Trump." (Short answer: people there are white, feel "left behind," and blame Obama.)

In the months before West Virginia's May 7 primary, there was a second national spotlight on the Mountain State. It followed the long-awaited criminal trial of Don Blankenship, the CEO of the coal giant Massey Energy, for his role in the explosion of an underground mine in Raleigh County that killed twenty-nine miners. The six-month trial ended in early April when a federal judge convicted the CEO on a single count of conspiracy to violate federal mine safety standards and sentenced him to one year in minimum-security prison. Outside the courthouse, a family member of one of the mine explosion victims expressed his grieving outrage over the paltry sentence to a local TV reporter. The interview was a minor viral hit, briefly humanizing and thus complicating Trump's Palin-esque promises to "mine, baby, mine."

The interview, and the Blankenship trial generally, complicated Trump's coal boosterism because it opened a window onto the gritty realities of the mining economy: Coal jobs were never all that great, even in the union heyday. West Virginia was always poor, with the highest mortality rates in the country. Trump clearly did not understand the forces that killed local mining economies, any more than he understood why so many West Virginians have always fled in search of other kinds of work, or why some locals were agitating not for more mining, but a stop to the decapitation of its mountains and the poisoning of its land, air, and water.

There was a time when Trump intuited all this. In a 1990 *Playboy* interview, a forty-three-year-old Trump was asked about the rush he gets from "doing a deal." He responded, "It's my canvas. I like the challenge and tell the story of the coal miner's son. The coal miner gets black lung disease, his son gets it, then his son. If I had been the son of a coal miner, I would have left the damn mines. But most people don't have the imagination—or whatever—to leave their mine. They don't have 'it.'"

In 2016 West Virginia, however, Trump established himself as the black lung candidate. He understood that even if miners hate coal dust and loathe the bosses, they hate those Democrats perceived as "anti-coal" even more. On one of his few remaining afternoons as a free man, Don Blankenship joined a group of miners in waving Trump signs and chanting "Coal! Coal! Coal! Coal!" outside of a Hillary Clinton campaign event in Williamson, Mingo County. (In 1921, Mingo County miners waged the Battle of Blair Mountain, among the biggest and bloodiest labor rebellions in American history.) In neighboring Logan County, local officials barred Clinton and her "anti-coal message" from appearing on County property.

"In West Virginia, time stands still, at best, and sometimes runs backwards, in hundred-year leaps," said Bob Kincaid, an online progressive talk radio host in Fayette County. "The miners bellow 'coal!' as if invoking some ancient and blood-thirsty god, never understanding that it's Wall Street, far more than any tepid regulations, who did in all those underground mining jobs. It's Wall Street that funds mountaintop removal, a process that needs far fewer people to get at the last dregs of Appalachian coal than does underground mining."

Trump did not mention Wall Street—or slack global demand, or the rise of gas, or mechanization—when he addressed a Charleston crowd of thirteen thousand two days before the West Virginia primary. Standing before a row of miners waving signs reading Trump Digs Coal, the candidate donned a hard hat gifted him by the West Virginia Coal Association (a trade group) and promised out-of-work and underemployed miners that soon "they'd be back to better than before," rescued by a coal revival that would keep the country safe from "the hands of OPEC." Over the course of an hour, he skated a wide, artful circle around King Coal's dirty open secret: it's not industry profits that are down for the count, but unionized mining employment.

The Trump campaign saw Charleston as a fitting location for the candidate's first energy speech as the Republican nominee. Days earlier, the GOP primary season had effectively ended when Trump's last two rivals conceded following his victory in Indiana. In the Hoosier State, Trump used the closing of a Carrier plant the way he used the shuttering of mines in West Virginia: as a symbol of globalist, elitist betrayal. But while his version of the Carrier story carried the punch of truth, Trump's coal story was a clumsy cover and a con.

Traveling through the state's gutted hollows, I met people who knew this full well, but planned to vote for Trump anyway. Their number included the most famous anti-coal activist in Raleigh County.

* * *

Ed Wiley is a fifty-nine-year-old retired mineworker. Though he has the face of an older man, framed by a long gray chin-curtain style beard, he still has ripped upper arms and Popeye forearms. He has a quiet philosophical manner and piercing blue eyes. Like a lot of West Virginia men, what he loves most is turkey hunting. Lately a pinched leg nerve and back issues have kept him out of the woods and off his feet in the same Coal Creek house where he grew up and now lives with his wife, Debbie. That eponymous creek runs past Wiley's front yard. Like all moving water in the area, mining runoff poisoned it beyond use ages ago. So long ago, and so thoroughly, there's never been need for warning signs.

Even as a kid, Wiley never liked the idea of working down in the cold, dark mines. He chose a career above ground, doing strip work on surface mines. He didn't think much about the health impacts of the coal industry until 2004, when his granddaughter Kayla complained of feeling sick. When her illness persisted, Wiley began looking into the respiratory ailments that plagued not only his own kin but many other students at Marsh Fork Elementary. He realized the widespread illnesses undoubtedly stemmed from the area's torrent of toxic coal waste, which sent a steady mist of silica dust and other chemicals down onto the school. Wiley began a crusade to have the school relocated, linking up with a fledgling local activist group, Coal River Mountain Watch. When industry and state officials ignored him—"They just couldn't admit it was dangerous"—Wiley announced plans to walk from Coal Creek to Washington, DC, where he would directly petition the secretary of education and Robert Byrd, the West Virginia senator who was then in the twilight of his legendary career.

Thus began an unlikely second career as an activist, taking Wiley to the nation's capital and beyond. A decade ago, Mike Roselle, the veteran activist who co-founded Earth First! and the Rainforest Action Network, moved a few houses down from Wiley to help lead the fight against mountaintop removal. Roselle describes the miner-turned-activist as "the single best grassroots organizer I have ever seen."

Early one morning, I sat down with Wiley in the small tool shed he calls his "pout house." With his yellow Labrador stretched out at his feet, he talked about coal, Trump, and a future for West Virginia without coal.

"My family's been up here in this hollow, probably around three hundred and fifty years. I never did leave. Stayed right here. It's been pretty good. It's beautiful country. I met my wife, and here I am.

"I didn't work down in the mines. Ain't for me. It weren't for my dad. I worked around the faces of the mines, did ground work, strip job work. It was seventeen hours a day a lot of times, seven days a week. The money was more than I ever made before. I had a medical card I'd never had before. But I'd never do it again. It ain't worth it. The money—unless you got ahold of yourself—the more you make, the more you spend. I've seen these guys, they kind of get above their raisins. Then it bottoms out, and here they got a home, cars, four-wheelers they're trying to pay for. You don't need a bass boat all the time.

"I can understand the pride of the deep miners. It's a dangerous job. Nasty. Dangerous. I've been down in that hole. What I don't understand, after all these years, a hundred years—it's one of the worst jobs. Why would you want this job? Why wouldn't you want something better? They won't let go. They won't accept something better. I don't know why. This area down here is one of the toughest bunch of people I've ever seen. Hard headed.

"The new [coal economy] isn't like the old. There's millions and millions of dollars that leaves out of here every day, but never gets put back into the towns no way, shape, or form. Look at Whitesville. I've seen pictures of that town back in the '40s. It was booming. *Booming*. Couldn't park nowhere. Everything open. Booming. And they was still digging it out by hand, you know what I'm saying? Now you look at the amount of coal that leaves out of here, and that town is dead. Dead. There's something wrong somewhere.

"This mayor that's down there now in Whitesville, when he first got in, three or four years ago, he tried to [get the coal company to reinvest in the local economy] but the company slapped him down. They told the coal miners to move their bank account to another bank so it wouldn't be in Whitesville. The coal company was going to take *their* money out of Whitesville Bank because the mayor was bucking on them. They put him in his place. He just rolled up. They let that town die. Millions of dollars go through it—and nothing [comes back]. Now they want to try to restore it, wanting to turn it into like a 'Coal Mining Historical Something Town.' Why? That's what killed your town.

"There's a lot of things we could do here. When they do this stripping here [*points in the direction of a decapitated mountain*], all that timber got pushed in big piles and burnt. That could have been turned into toys, furniture, anything. That's jobs there. That's jobs. They wouldn't even let the pulp people get it out of there because they couldn't get it out fast enough. They could've turned it into chip board and stuff. But they wouldn't let the timber people get it out. They weren't fast enough. They just shove it in a pile and bury it, burn it.

"There's jobs in coal, but look at other states that don't have coal. What do they do? How are they making it? West Virginia University just moved some people out here, in Beckley. It was on TV a little while ago, they're going to get some training going, help retrain people.

"The coal miners get up on TV, I don't know if the companies are paying them to say this—they get up on TV, and say, 'If I can't do coal I can't do nothing. I don't know anything else.' Buddy, you're wrong. You guys are some of the smartest guys in West Virginia. They could do about anything. If

72

they've never done it, you show them once and they'll do it. Why would they say that? Here you are, a high school graduate, some of them's college graduates. Some of them's got engineer degrees. If you want people to come to West Virginia and bring jobs here, you don't want people sitting up there saying, 'Well I don't know nuthin.' You couldn't pay me to get up there and say that. That's a disgrace to West Virginia. To get up on TV—it's not right. I don't like it. Why disgrace yourself like that when you know you're smarter than that? We could do lots of things.

"The Big Branch explosion [leading to Don Blankenship's conviction] made the miners prouder. The saddest part about it is, people lost their fathers and people lost sons. Some of them settled right off the bat for $3.5 million. I know some of these people. My buddy Irv, his sister lost a husband. They took this money, and I don't know what they've done. Some people, like the Coles, built this great big stone house. Well, if you look out at the hollow, there's the strip job. They built a mansion of a house up in this little hollow. But you look out the door and you can see the strip job. They're stripping in his back yard and wanting to come around both sides of him. It's his business to do it that way. It's his son's money. Lost a son. But we ain't seen one dime of that money go into these communities. Why not say, 'I got $3.5 million, I'm going to take a million and build a packaging factory.' Something to create jobs, so nobody else's kids got to go back into a coal mine. I haven't seen nothing like that happening in this community. Not even an ice cream shop. Not even a little, tiny mom-and-pop ice cream shop. That upsets me.

"I know everybody up and down this river. Hunted with them, worked with them, hung out with them, all kind of stuff. Since the school [pollution] issue, they don't hardly look at me now. People won't talk to me, won't come around.

You go out to the store, you might get a nod or a wave out of them. You really thought they was your best buddy at one time. You know? You find out who your friends are when something like this happens. You really do.

"I went up against the company for their kids too. I made that clear a lot of times. This ain't just *my* granddaughter. I'm standing up and speaking for all the kids. Nobody else will, I'll be their voice. Once I'd seen, and learnt, and did some research and stuff, I knew it was a bad place for kids. It was a bad place for anybody. Still is.

"When I worked the mines, I was blinded by the money and the medical card I never had. I worked behind my granddaughter's school. I didn't even think about it. My granddaughter was down there. Never thought nothing of it until she was sick. All the time, that silica dust. You can't see it. It's a really fine particle. Well, sure the company knew. They didn't care. There were a lot of violations, two hundred and some violations. It wasn't just the dust. If [the dam holding the waste] failed, nine hundred and seventy-seven lives would be perished. Three hundred kids. In seconds. No time to evacuate.

"When Kayla got sick, I worked on it for about a week. I called Channel 5 [WDTV, the CBS affiliate in Weston, West Virginia], and turned out at the school, did an interview. I didn't even know Coal River Mountain Watch existed in Whitesville. I drove right by it every day working down there. Didn't even know. They'd been watching that school too. They said, "Let's get together." So we did.

"Two years later, and we done about everything we could do. I couldn't sleep at night. I'm just sitting down here, and I got to thinking, 'Senator Byrd.' He's about ready to retire. He's in his last term. He is who he is. You can't hurt his name. It won't hurt him to shake this boat and help these kids. I said, 'Well, why don't you announce that we're going to Senator

Byrd's house? Take the news straight to the man.' Go down to the capital, do a press thing. I'm thinking, 'I'll do that. I'm ready to go right now. That'll shake them up maybe.' Left within a month's time.

"Met a lot of good people on the walk. Every town I come to, I went to the mayor's office. Handed my pamphlets to everybody, put a pamphlet in every mailbox. I got in trouble for that [*chuckles*]. I was handing out too many pamphlets. Everybody got a pamphlet. If somebody would be on their front porch, believe it, I'd walk up. Everybody got a pamphlet.

"I met with Byrd in the Hart Senate Building. Byrd stood right there next to the big poster I carried all over the country. It's a full-sized poster, aerial view of the school, and you'd point and show everything out. Had that in there, and pointed and described everything that was going on, plain and simple to him. Byrd was from this area, he's from the Daniels area. I just made it kind of clear to him: these are your people. Somewhere down there, you're bound to have some kind of kinfolk. This is your territory, Raleigh County area. I thought he'd do something. I figured he would do more than what he did. I kept writing letters to him. He said it was a county and state issue, not a federal. Nothing he could do. He called Blankenship and Massey a 'rogue coal company'. Well, what coal company ain't never been a rogue coal company? You tell me what's not.

"A little colored boy from New York died for the campaign. There was a [special-needs] school up in the Bronx, one of the teachers got involved to help me raise money. There was one class that was leading this. They brought in pennies, had a chart, keeping count. This one particular little boy, a little African American boy, he had asthma real bad. He had a bad attack this particular night before the collection ended. He made it through the night okay. He wouldn't go to the doctor. He got to school, the first thing he done, was take his pennies. That's all he cared about. Then he sat down in his chair and took a real bad asthma attack there. Made it to the hospital, and passed away. At the hospital, they said [to his parents], 'Why didn't you bring him?' They said, 'Because he wanted to come and get his pennies in.' [*long pause.*] That whole class was special little kids. They knew everything about the story. One little girl wanted to come up on stage with me. She was four feet tall. Arms maybe an inch around. She put her little fist up, and yelled, 'All I want to say, is to you Governor [Joe] Manchin, you're a bad governor. You better help them little kids!' You know, you're sitting there and your heart is going out.

"That class encouraged the whole school to get involved, talking about environmental issues. They were the first people to give money—was those little kids from New York. They raised $650. They were the poor kids. Then I had what I called the 'richie kids.' There's a school, two blocks above Trump's office, where the park is, a private Catholic school, big old place. I'd go up there and meet with them kids twice a year. Take 'em in the park and show 'em different plants and such. The 'richie kids,' they wasn't comin' up with nothing. It was the poor kids, they were the only ones that gave money."

I asked Wiley what kind of Raleigh County he'd like to leave for his grandchildren. "They can do a lot around here." There's a lot to save. It's a beautiful area. You get out towards Arlington and all that, anywhere with Civil War battles. Well, shoot, that's the prettiest place, it's protected, they get extra money and all that. Well, they was Civil War people down in here, too! I like to see this get turned into a big national park myself, and the jobs that would go with it.

"They're talking about jobs, so-called 'reclaim and fix' what the coal companies tore up, but none of that ever happened. They're using the ruined mountains for military practice. They said they couldn't find nowhere else better than Raleigh County mining sites that resembled Iraqi terrain. They're landing cargo planes and taking off, practicing dropping stuff out the back. I was going to go up there and hang up a great big plywood sign: 'Iraq: Five miles' [*laughs*]. I don't like it. I really don't. People say, 'Well, at least they're using it for something.'

"I think they want everybody out of this valley. See, there's seams of coal underneath here, underneath this river, that goes all the way to Chesapeake down past Charleston. I've seen them strip a big valley like this in Pennsylvania. They gutted it. I mean, they gutted it. They started consolidating schools. Then they started shutting post offices down. No schools, no post offices. Then you look at Whitesville. You got to go all the way down to Charleston from Whitesville to get anything.

"Trump will get elected. I'm for it. I said it from the beginning, when everybody said I was crazy. People in America like his attitude. We're tired of being broke. People's tired of bull crap. Jobs never should have never left here. They should have stayed in America. He's a businessman, and mostly everything in the world now depends on some kind of business. We need to keep our butts at home, stay out of these wars. That's the sort of thing you'd have to watch with him, is can he keep himself calm? Control of his bipolar. That might be what we need, is a good bipolar president [*laughs*]. He says it like it is. If he says it, he's probably going to do it one way or another, or try to. He don't hold nothing back. That's for sure. He probably knows people all over the place. Can make some kind of jobs happen.

"But they need to quit talking about that border wall shit. I never did like this. The drugs are going to get here from somewhere, one way or another. We don't need a damn wall. Get along with the people. Bring them and build more. Help us build the country. They want to work too. Let's put them to work. Put everybody to work. You look at all the problems it's caused in California right now—it's over that damn wall. We need to just work this out on that. We need to get that straightened out so people ain't fighting in the street.

"And Trump should stop calling them scoundrels. Everybody's not a scoundrel. And them people are desperate. You become a bit of a scoundrel when you get desperate, whether you are or not. You get hungry, you're going to grab that donut, if you can get it."

* * *

West Virginia's flip from blue to red in presidential elections did not happen overnight, but one night in particular has come to symbolize that transformation. On October 31, 2000, the actor Charlton Heston spoke to a packed house at the armory in Beckley, the seat of Raleigh County. Speaking on behalf of the National Rifle Association, Heston urged West Virginia to buck history and vote for George W. Bush and Dick Cheney. "Mr. Gore has the guts of a guppy," Heston told an audience full of miners and their families. "If Al Gore is elected, he will have the power to hammer your gun rights. . . . Freedom has never seen greater peril or needed you more urgently to come to her defense." That week, the state supported the Republican presidential candidate for the first time since 1984.

If people outside of West Virginia have heard anything about Raleigh County, it probably isn't about Heston's visit to Beckley, but about the nearby town of Oceana, the subject of the acclaimed 2013 documentary, *Oxyana*, a chronicle of the area's opioid epidemic. Everyone in the area talks about the drugs. This includes a Trump supporter and former industrial engineer named Lenny Massimino, proprietor of one of the few non–chain businesses still open in Beckley. When I stopped by his auto parts store one afternoon, he pulled a stool up to the counter and we spoke as a television in the corner played Fox News.

"When I met my wife at West Virginia University in 1979, this was a great place to raise a family. If you told me back then there'd be drug a problem in southern West Virginia, I'd say, 'Son, you need to go back to New York.' Oh, they were going to drink and raise hell, pot smoking, but hell, that's everywhere. But the oxycodone, the heroin, and all that . . . It's bad. You see it everyday, they walk in here, blurry eyed. A lot of older people, too. They've lost where they're going, so they end up with drugs.

"The six counties in southern West Virginia are in a depression. Not in a recession, a depression. The base everything was built on got knocked out. Nobody is working. Nobody's got any money. There's no people. It's what happens when the EPA tells you, 'Shut every coal-fired power plant down in the United States.' If you want other [sorts of business] to come in, you have to do it slowly. You just can't turn off a switch. They talk about climate change. The only one that controls the thermostat on this good green earth of ours is the guy upstairs.

"Business is terrible, terrible. At one time, I had five stores, had four stores last April, before I closed my plywood store, right in the midst of coal country. A lot of coal mines are taking Chapter 11, Chapter 7. They used to be good accounts for us. You lose business you did monthly with them, and you lose all the people that worked for them, plus the money they owed you. It's been devastating. You can just see the traffic on

Route 3, the main drag through West Virginia. There's hardly any cars moving. You go into Walmart, you can park in the first row! Used to be you had to pack a lunch, you'd have to park so far back. A lot of the hotels and restaurants regain a bit during the summertime because we're a midway point for travelers going down to the beach and stuff. That helps. Plus, we get a lot of business from travelers breaking down.

"I was a Democrat until I turned fifty-nine years old [in 2008]. Voted for Jimmy Carter in 1976, Ronald Reagan in 1980. I think this year things need to be shook up. The establishments have gone way too far. All they worry about is K Street, their power structure, how to keep the counties around Washington, DC wealthy. Trump's a power person, but not a power broker in Washington. People are sick and tired of lobbyists, special interests. It's just a paid game. Small business, small people can't afford to hire a lobbyist.

"What you're seeing is an angry America. You're see-ing people voting now for Trump that hasn't voted forever. They're not complacent any more. Say he does win, and he can't get done what he wants to get done, then you're going to see another like him. We're tired of working our tails off for nothing. We're tired of all these promises on health insur-ance, and all you are doing is paying out more money. Your deductibles are sky-high, your insurance costs are sky-high. My wife is sixty-four and we got to buy maternity coverage. Come on, get real.

"Trump knows where we got to go. You know the old say-ing, nobody ever got a job from a poor man. What we need is an LBJ in Trump's clothing. LBJ knew every skeleton in Washington. He said, 'If you don't do what I want you to do, I'll let them know what you did.'

"We were talking about drugs. None of Trump's kids have drug issues. Those kids had a boatload of money available to them. He raised them right. Good men raise good children. He's a mouthy New Yorker, and if you know anybody from New York, they all got a line of bullshit [*laughs*]. That's the way they are. They'll argue with you about who's going to pay dinner. You know, they're just argumentative people. He's that way. You attack him, he's going to attack you back twice as hard, and be nasty and make you feel like a heel.

"I really got angry the other day watching the protests [at a Trump rally] in California. I'm not angry at them protesting. That's our rights. But when you are in America, son, don't protest under a frickin' Mexican flag. Trump explains things in the big picture, you know, 'build a wall.' I'm the great grandson of immigrants that came through Ellis Island. When they came here, there was no Italian flag flying over the house, okay? You weren't allowed to speak Italian in my grandmother's house. She would swear at me in Italian, but she wanted you to speak the language of this country, okay? That's the way it's supposed to be. A melting pot, you become an American. My father and uncles fought in WWII. They weren't Italians fighting other Italians. They were Americans, okay? We're losing that. Don't protest under a Mexican flag in America.

"We lost our basic industries in this country. We lost the industrial sector. Textiles. You can't find a shirt made in the United States anymore. If you do find one, you can't afford it. New York City, all them apartment buildings used to be textile plants, weaving and making shirts and making cloth. You had a rag market in New York. Manufacturing, boy, you got to look awful close to find it. The North Carolina furniture factories. The cotton mills that was down in the Carolinas. The steel mills in Pittsburgh. Where did they go?

"What bugs me about losing manufacturing, getting your hands dirty is looked down upon. When I grew up we weren't saying, 'Oh, God this is dirty, terrible!' We were saying, 'Hot damn, daddy works tomorrow!' And he made a good living and was able to educate his kids, was able to save, okay? Was able to have a good retirement for himself. Americans shouldn't be ashamed to get their hands dirty. The dirt that gets under your fingernails, my dad would tell me, is clean dirt. You worked for it and it washes off. A lot of this dirt we have in this nation is no longer clean dirt."

Chapter Five

New Mexico

I arrived in downtown Albuquerque just as protestors began to pool outside the city's convention center. Raucous, they flowed into the heavily policed space from downtown, where they'd marched and chanted under signs of spectrum spanning, anti-Trump insult: "Fascist . . . fuck face . . . man baby." Hours before the candidate was scheduled to speak, the familiar factions had arrived in force, from the exuberant Free Hug crowd, to sullen Black Bloc cadres quietly debating the security merits of bandanas versus Guy Fawkes masks. As dusk set in and the air turned cool, a thousand people chanted, sang, and laughed. A trumpeter played Mexican-flavored covers of patriotic American songs. It almost felt more like a party than a protest. Then the Trump people started showing up.

To get to the Albuquerque Convention Center, rally goers had to walk fifty yards down a narrow pathway created by waist-high metal barriers. There was no buffer between this pathway and the protestors, who filled its length like an Oscars night paparazzi line of verbal punishment. Most attendees bowed their heads and adopted a brisk pace while passing under the torrent of taunts and shouts of "Shame on you!" Some attendees returned fire, creating some tense scenes. Albuquerque police called for reinforcements from around the state before doors opened on Trump's seven o'clock speech.

Inside the convention area, an enormous line formed alongside dozens of merch dealers anxious to clear inventory ahead of the looming end of primary season. They walked the line with Trump tie-dyes, baseball hats, and an array of anti-Hillary gear. One button, new on the market, announced a "KFC Hillary Special: 2 Fat Thighs, 2 Small Breasts . . . Left Wing." While perusing these offerings, I heard the unmistakable laugh of Mark Spence, the Trump parking lot super-fan from Texas I met on a freezing morning in Racine, Wisconsin, handing out flyers with links to Paul Harvey radio monologues. He was wearing star-spangled face paint and seemed genuinely happy to see me, but apologized for having to run. The line was now moving into the building, and it was a long overnight drive to Anaheim, where Trump was speaking the following afternoon. "My father spent the last twenty years of his life in Orange County, so it has a special energy for me," he said, flashing a big all-dentures smile.

As the back half of the line neared the metal detectors, a white protestor in his twenties entered the convention area and began screaming within shouting distance of rally goers. "You're all fucking welfare cases!" he yelled, prowling back and forth like an enraged lion. "You just don't want anyone else getting any! You're all a bunch of fucking frauds! Donald Trump is a fraud!"

Only two people heckled back at the protestor, telling him to "Get a job." They were Eldon and Theo Martinez, father and son Trump fans from the Acoma Indian Reservation. Eldon, the father, was a rancher and retired Albuquerque cop. Theo had recently completed a decade in the Army. I asked what they thought of the protest across the street.

"Half those people are illegal immigrants," said Theo. "I went to war and fought for this? Served nine and a half years? To have them protest and call me names?"

I asked if Trump was popular on the reservation. The elder Martinez said that he was. "The black man has had eight years to turn the economy around, and he failed," he said. "Most people believe the federal government gives Native Americans handouts. That's not true. We provide for ourselves. We live off the land. We raise cattle. Many Acoma were farmers. But it's dwindled. Now, most Acoma work for private businesses. The biggest issue on the reservation is unemployment. It has always been unemployment. Why not give Mr. Trump the opportunity to bring the country back? Who better than Trump, a business owner who has failed a couple of times? Who knows how to pick himself up and move forward?"

Thirty minutes later, the candidate addressed eight thousand supporters while standing in front of the New Mexico state flag. During those parts of Trump's speech where he sounds most like a dime-store Midtown Mussolini, I found unpleasant mental exercise in imagining the flag's symbol—an Indian sun nestled in the conquistador cross of Habsburg Spain—as a bold red ensign of an It-Happened-Here America. As he always does, Trump addressed the fascism fears of his critics with unprompted and over-compensatory claims that his campaign is a "love fest." Between interruptions by protestors, he rolled through his primary speech, putting a border-state emphasis on the Mexican smugglers he said were driving the national heroin epidemic (as opposed to the Big Pharma painkillers responsible for nine out of ten opioid addictions). Political reporters seized on his criticism of New Mexico's notably absent Republican governor, Susan Martinez. "Your governor has got to do a better job," Trump said to cheers.

No matter what Trump said, the biggest news out of Albuquerque was still bound to be the *Sturm und Drang* on the streets. While Trump delivered his speech, protestors rushed the police line, ransacking the wares of fleeing vendors and setting one of the tables afire. With the police buffer outside the entrance in chaos, the security team directed everyone to a back exit, struggling to be heard over the theme of *Space Jam*, Trump's outro music ("Y'all ready for this?"). Windows along the convention center's escalator and pristine plant-dotted hallways revealed smoke and prowling protestors beyond the glass. George Romero fans leaving the rally must have thought of the zombie-infested parking lot outside the *Dawn of the Dead* shopping mall. Apprehension competed with post-rally jubilation. I heard one man say, "Well, I can cross that off my bucket list. All that's left is going over Niagara Falls in a barrel."

As the crowd dispersed onto the city's sidewalks, some rally goers waded toward the protest zone, which by now was encroaching the perimeter of the convention center. The night filled with the sounds of racially charged shouting matches. "Go back to Mexico!" "The border is that way!" "Come at me, bro!" "Where's that white boy that said that?" In the streets, the protest rolled by in the full flower of Western car culture: a parade of tricked-out trucks with thirty-six-inch rims, revved engines, and burned rubber as girls in tight tops rode the sun roofs waving Mexican flags and screaming "Fuck Trump!" A few trucks blasted rapper Nipsey Hussle's campaign anthem, "FDT (Fuck Donald Trump)."

I sat on the steps of a 7-Eleven at Fourth Street and Copper Avenue and drank a cup of coffee. A few feet away, a white Trump fan in his late thirties silently took in the acrid and acrimonious scene. He was Joe Sookov, a paramedic and recent Albuquerque transplant from Nevada. He shook his head and gestured toward the street. "This is what happens when you have a challenge to the establishment and there's a forty-six percent Hispanic population," he said. "As soon as my kids finish high school, I'm moving to Arizona. Sheriff Joe runs a tight county. The Hispanics are, uh, a little more in check over there."

I finished my coffee and returned to the convention center, where clashes with police went past midnight, long after the last rally-goer had gone home to bed.

* * *

The next morning, I drove south, toward the border. During the drive, I listened to talk radio seethe over what Albuquerque police termed the previous night's "riot." Trump had waited until morning to comment, tweeting, "The protesters in New Mexico were thugs who were flying the Mexican flag. The rally inside was big and beautiful, but outside, criminals." Scott Stiegler, a popular local host, was livid over the police restraint. So, too, was Milwaukee Sheriff David Clarke, sitting in for the nationally syndicated Glenn Beck. Clarke berated the police for not "taking the gloves off" and going on the offensive. Neither host mentioned a crucial bit of background to this restraint: a 2014 federal investigation that uncovered rampant abuse and unwarranted use of lethal force by the Albuquerque PD, resulting in a federal monitor.

I was driving toward the state's borderlands, the site of the proposed Wall that remained the central promise and metaphor of Trump's campaign. I stopped along the way in Truth or Consequences, a hot-springs town that renamed itself in 1950 after a popular radio and TV quiz show. Just past the exit, graffiti scrawled on a makeshift billboard declared, We Don't Trust Hillary. Another handmade sign announced the local GOP headquarters. I entered to find a gaunt fellow named Clint Langdon seated glumly at a desk. "I'm gonna vote for him, but I don't like him or trust him one bit," he said of Trump. "You know who you should talk to, is Gerald LaFont, over in Elephant Butte. He's big on Trump."

I found the pot-bellied LaFont behind the bar at the Elephant Butte Inn. LaFont bought the hotel in 1996, banking on a steady flow of regional tourists seeking summer relief in the cool temperatures of southern New Mexico's high desert. The big draw is Elephant Butte Lake, which in recent years has been losing water to extended drought and a water-sharing agreement with Texas. The agreement, negotiated by former governor Bill Richardson, is much resented by locals. "Why did Richardson sign it? Because he's Mexican!" Clint Langdon told me back in Truth or Consequences.

A proud son of New Mexico, LaFont welcomed the chance to sit and talk about Trump, the weather, climate change, and local history.

"I grew up during the 1940s, the son of an Indian trader," he said. "I was raised on the Navajo reservation, the biggest reservation in the country. It goes over into Arizona and touches up in Utah. We operated the trading post in Prewitt, between Gallup and Grants, fourteen miles off the

Continental Divide. We traded Indians [*laughs*]. No, we didn't. Years ago, the Indians didn't have a source of food or goods they needed. The trading post provided everything. There was around thirty traders. Your posts were in outlying areas, maybe five to ten miles from where the Indians lived. They'd come on wagons, trade, and then go home in a day's time. There was no money involved. It was usually pledging sheep and buying wool. Then the trader would give the family credit so they could buy food. We'd go out, gather the sheep in the fall, take and sack the wool. It was a family deal. We all worked. The only day we closed was on Christmas Day. On that day, we varnished the sandstone floors. As the Indians began buying cars and trucks, and got jobs, they didn't need us anymore. The posts faded away about 1952, '53, '54.

"The Indians never really accepted the traders. We were friendly, we all got along good, but they'll never invite you to dinner. It's their culture. It's just one of those things. You get used to it. They don't think the way we think. It's just like Bush being in Iraq there. Best thing he could have done was said, 'Adios, guys.' Because those people do not think the way we think. You could have a democracy, you could have any goddamn thing you want over there, and they think the way they think and they're not going to change. Indians are the same way.

"When I bought this place in 1996, it was a dump. I tore everything out, rebuilt it. Until 2001, we had good business. September 11 hurt businesses throughout the country. Then we started doing pretty good again, until Mr. Richardson let all of our water out in 2004. That changed everything. The other thing that kills us is the press we get out of Albuquerque. It's negative, 'Drought! The water's down!' Everybody thinks there's no water here. We still have the biggest lake in the state of New Mexico. It's really quite usable almost all year round. There are times it's up, times it's down. This year it's up quite a ways and it's doing well. But the press is not very nice to us down here. Lately, we've been drawing more people out of Texas than Albuquerque. We get a lot of military people. When it comes to West Texas, this is the closest lake."

I ask LaFont if he thinks climate change has something to do with extended drought in recent years. "I don't know if you know it, but this planet has been going through space for a long, long time," he said. "Did you know this place had ice all over it at one time? And do you remember where the oceans came from? Well, hell, trees need carbon monoxide. If we had more carbon monoxide, we might have more trees. A lot of the climate change stuff comes from intelligent people that sit in universities and never been anywhere and don't know a damn thing. Gosh, here in New Mexico we've had volcanoes. We've got the ice caves over there. The world has changed. It's going to keep changing.

LaFont segued to Trump, and why he liked him, warts and all. "Trump's a businessman. That's what I like about him. And he's not part of the establishment. The American people are sick and tired of the establishment. He's probably got ten times more balls than Obama's got. I do have a problem with anybody that talks about themselves. Being a businessman and relatively successful, I don't think you need to let everybody know everything about you. That's where I come from. I don't think he's exactly what I would call 'smart' in things that he just blurts out. It's sort of like when a bunch of guys are sitting at the bar talking, it just comes out. I think he should be more methodical about it. There's a lot of people like Rush Limbaugh that thinks he *shouldn't* change. Well, that's fine, but I think more people would be more open to him if he was a little bit more selective in what he says."

I asked if he thought Trump could win New Mexico, a border swing state, in November. "Up here, the border situation doesn't seem to bother us," he replied. "We really can't tell the difference. Most of the people, they just go right on by to Albuquerque. The only thing we have here is the people that run out of money and sit down outside Walmart and ask for food. This is a funny state. It's primarily Democrat, and major Hispanic, no matter what anybody says. The state is pretty much controlled by the Hispanic people up around Espanola and that northern part of the state. Whether anybody likes it or not. Of course they've been here five and six generations, too. So they're kind of inbred to that way of thinking. You and I aren't going to change it. As far as my predictions are concerned, I don't know. Looks like Hillary's got her tit in a wringer. I wonder how that happened? [*laughs*]"

I ask if he'd seen the reports about what happened in Albuquerque the night before. "That was a bunch of bullshit. The policemen and the state of New Mexico should have been ready and not let it happen. I graduated from Albuquerque High School in 1958. We didn't have the strife between the Hispanics and the whites that we have now. If anybody got out of hand, they got the shit beat out of them. You didn't burn the American flag. You didn't even think about it. Where I grew up, everybody had a gun. I had a gun when I was ten years old. But you just lived differently in those days. A lot of the problems today have to do with attitude. A lot of them act the way they do because they know they can get by with it."

LaFont veered into a long disquisition on the Indian fighter Kit Carson and how he brought the local Navajo clans to heel. Taking my leave, I thanked LaFont for the history lesson and wished him luck in weathering what may be many years of deepening drought.

"I've been doing this for over fifty years," he said. "When you're dumb, you got to be tough."

* * *

I drove south on a stretch of the old Route 66 that cuts through the Acoma and Laguna Indian reservations. Amid an ocean of desert scrub, I slowed while passing a ramshackle trailer compound, where a man was standing at an outdoor work-table. He looked out of place in a baseball cap, purple T-shirt tucked into jeans, and Nike running shoes. I approached the wire fence separating his property from the road and asked him what he was doing. He said, "Making a windmill." He introduced himself as Mike, declining to give his last name. He was voting Trump, he said, and had recently adopted a life in the desert to pursue his life's mission: a breakthrough in micro-scale alternative energy.

"I was living in Albuquerque when I moved down here to work on my little windmill," he said. "I needed a place to build the prototype and test it. This was the perfect place: lots of wind, nobody to gripe about what I'm doing. So I'm out here roughing it until I get it going. I've got a little solar shower. I haul my water. As you can tell, I'm about five miles past the last power line. You know, the mother of invention is necessity. Out here, if I want power, I have to make it.

"I've been thinking about green energy a long time. Solar was over my head, so I decided to go with wind. I'm tinkering with a model. The only thing that I'm purchasing from an outside vendor is the actual generator. Why reinvent the wheel? One of the markets I'm going to invest in is the res-ervations. The Indians got folk further out than me from power. And let's face it, we keep sending our military into places it shouldn't be for oil. We need other kinds of power for people. I hope I can find niche markets like around here, with strong winds. Make a buck or two.

"These winds in high desert, it's a problem for little turbines, for micro-wind. The generators burn out because of the occasional eighty- or ninety- mile-an-hour gust. What I tried to do, and I think I accomplished with this new one, once I assemble it, is limit the RPMs so it won't burn out the generator. I got my fingers crossed. I got to go back into Albuquerque next week and pick up some parts I'm having manufactured there. Then I'll stick it up and hope it survives the wind gusts. That's what I'm doing out here. Just trying to work a windmill."

I tell him I understand how the desert plains winds could be a problem. More than once, they'd blown my compact rental car clear across the blacktop like a cotton willow. I ask him how long he's been interested in the engineering challenges of green energy.

"It's been in my head for a long, long time," he said. "When I was in the Navy, I worked on aircrafts and that kind of thing. This was during Vietnam. When I got out, I worked in machine shops, weld shops. I'd see something an engineer had designed, I'd look at it, and think, 'I can do better than that.' But I just kind of kicked around. Life happens. Finally, I stopped drinking and went back to school. Finished a two-year business degree. Got my priorities straight. Once I did that, I couldn't get the turbine out of my head. I finally decided, okay, I need to either make it work, or stop tinkering with it and walk away. So I bought this place and put one together. The first one didn't work. Went back and studied some more. Now I'm trying again. I'm out here until I decide it's a dream or a nightmare come true. I've been putting a lot of energy and money into it. I'm hoping at some point I can get a grant to help me proceed, or maybe take it to market."

I ask him what he thinks about Trump's pro–coal energy politics, his climate-change denial, and his opposition to government investment to spur the growth of a green energy sector.

"Trump gets a bad rap about a lot of things. You know, if you can prove to them that it's a money-making deal, that there's going to be a need for this, then businesspeople like Trump will invest. It's a free country. Nobody says, 'Put him in jail because he's got a windmill.' I don't foresee that ever happening. I don't need a federal program. I'll make them and sell them, or I won't. But, if there's a place that I can get a little grant money, I'd sure take that at this juncture. I don't worry about the government programs, the tax credits and all that. If it's a viable product, it will sell, and if not . . . The climate change stuff, well, I've concluded that when the cacti stop blooming and die, we might have a problem. But this is an arid area. It's dry. I don't believe them when they're talking about drought in New Mexico. Before the white man got out here and started planting things that needed more water, there was enough water. There still is. The snakes don't seem to mind it. The rattlers are okay."

I ask him if he trusts Trump, who was already beginning to pivot away from or soften earlier statements as he headed toward the general election. "I'm hoping that he's as conservative as he says he is. He used to be liberal on a lot of things. That's life. Over the years I've changed my mind about a lot of things. If I held the same viewpoints I did when I was younger, I'd be living in Colorado right now, rolling one fat one after another. But like I said, I'm just out here trying to get this done. Just me and a couple of rabbits. And the rattlesnakes. This here is just fabulous rattlesnake habitat. I try to stay in the open area and wear gaiters when I get out in the weeds and chop sage. Hopefully we have a live-and-let-live understanding. They do seem a little more cranky than last year. I don't know why. I ask them. They don't tell me."

I thanked him for the reminder to watch out for rattlers during roadside rest stops, and let him get back to work. Getting into my car, I asked him if he had a name picked out for his invention. "Oh, I'm already on name number ten," he said. "It's harder than you think, naming a windmill."

* * *

When the city of Deming was founded in 1881, residents boasted of a "New Chicago" in the southwest. The site of an intercontinental railroad crossing, a port of entry for neighboring Mexico—how could it do anything but boom? New Chicago never happened. Deming instead achieved a modest twentieth-century prosperity built upon agriculture. But over the years, like so many places, Deming—with a Latino-majority population of fifteen thousand—has seen its prosperity slide into disrepair and depopulation. One hundred and thirty-five years after the celebratory driving of its silver spike, Deming can boast only of a nation-leading teen pregnancy rate and a brief cameo in Cormac McCarthy's *The Crossing*.

On a row of mostly empty buildings in a downtown that looks like a Western movie set, a crude window painting of Uncle Sam marks Deming's GOP headquarters. I entered to find a retired realtor named Keith Harris exchanging good-byes with a middle-aged Latina woman. The woman was part of what Harris said was a historic wave for Luna County's outnumbered Republicans. "Because of Trump," he said, "we're growing for the first time in memory, registering more people than ever. This county is seventy percent Hispanic. A lot of them are changing over for Trump. We're registering new voters, the kind of people that never vote, or haven't voted since Reagan. We're up ten percent, a huge amount for this county."

What's "huge" for Luna County doesn't translate into many voters in absolute terms, and Harris conceded there is no national trend in Latinos defecting from the Democratic Party. But there are some, in New Mexico and elsewhere, willing to look past Trump's incendiary comments if they think he'll be good for the economy. "We have twenty percent unemployment. So do other towns," he said.

Harris isn't native to the area. He retired to Deming's dry climate from California, where he earned a PhD in history at UC-Berkeley in the '50s—"Before the pinkos took over," he joked—and made a small fortune in real estate. He framed Trump's candidacy in a larger context of American decline and the failed liberalism of both parties. "This year is a do-or-die election for the country," he said. "The border down in Hidalgo County is wide open. Drugs are pouring across. Human trafficking. Trump says it like most of us believe, about a lot of things."

When I expressed interest in meeting Trump supporters on the border, he pulled out his phone. "You know who you need to talk to, is the Keelers," he said. "Trump supporters. They know that border better than anyone. They can tell you stories."

He wrote down a phone number and wished me luck. As I got up to leave, he told me to take some of the literature piled and racked around the office. I grabbed a pamphlet titled, "The Communist Party Is the Democratic Party," and the Spring 2016 issue of *AMAC Advantage*, the membership magazine of a conservative "seniors advocacy group" that supports private retirement accounts and a higher retirement age. On the cover, Donald Trump leaned forward in a gilded Victorian chair surrounded by lush carpeting and vaunted ceilings supported by gold-trimmed marble pillars. Beside him, Melania struck a pose in a pink satin toga. The story promised to "unravel the mystery behind his successful campaign."

* * *

Murray and Judith Keeler live in isolation at the end of a long, unpaved road that twists deep into the Peloncillo Mountains. Their ranch sits among hills as rough and dangerous as can be found in New Mexico's remote southwestern boot. The area is well-known for crisscrossing smuggling routes out of Mexico. They've had friends killed and hijacked by smugglers; their home is frequently burglarized. Both grew up working on ranches and farms in southern New Mexico, and raised their six children the same. Murray Keeler, sixty-nine, is of slight build, with a coughing smoker's laugh and a face of tough sun-beaten leather. Judith, sixty-four, is ginger-haired and quietly ebullient, her fairer skin splotchy from a lifetime in the desert sun.

Over glasses of water at the Keeler's kitchen table, they spoke wistfully of the *braceros* they knew as children, laborers from Mexico named for the old program to replace farm workers lost during World War II. Terminated in 1964, the program is often invoked with nostalgia in border communities and held up as a model for an expanded guest worker program.* The Keelers also talked about their

---

* Less discussed are the rampant labor violations and human rights abuses that define H-2B guest worker programs. See the Southern Poverty Law Center's 2013 report, "Close to Slavery: Guestworker Programs in the United States."

frontline perspective on Donald Trump's Wall, their compassion for drug mules, and why the Border Patrol can be
a bigger pain in the ass than the cartels. I started by asking
about life in a major smuggling corridor. "We usually see
them after they've dropped their drugs and are on their
way back to Mexico," said Judith. "They stop by here for
food and water. We give it to them. I told Border Patrol, I
am going to feed them, because that's the way I was raised.
I'm not going to turn them in, because then you get in trouble with the cartels. Once, years ago, I turned a group in.
Border Patrol was bringing them back up here so I could
identify them when my neighbor met them on the road.
She said, 'Don't you take them back up there, because then
they'll know who turned them in.' After that, I don't turn
them in."

"They're pleasant enough when we're home," said Murray.
"If we're not here, they break in and take whatever they want.
We've had three break-ins in the last year. They robbed a
lot this last time, in February. They stole my binoculars, her
pistol, a chainsaw, all of my battery-powered drills. They're
on foot on the way back from dropping the drugs. There's at
least seventeen trails where they come up the Peloncillos and
drop off. Border Patrol has them mapped.

"The Border Patrol compound down the road there, it's a
farce. We tried to get them to build it down on the border. They
could have had a perfect view of the fence. But twenty miles
away? These are tough mountains. The US Army couldn't get
Geronimo out of these mountains. There are lots of ways they
can go. There's a trail they call Saint Mary's. It goes all the way
to Highway 9. Right now, Border Patrol counts Highway 9 as
the border. That's where they start working."

"Put them on the border. Like, right now," said Judith.
"We have another ranch in Hachita, five miles north of the

border. Our daughter, Amanda, is over there. One of the agents was telling her they can't stop the illegals until they cross Highway 9. The government, the bosses, whoever it is, won't let them stop them until after they get over there. Then they catch them, and can't keep them. Sometimes ICE [Immigration and Customs Enforcement] won't let them keep a guy, even if he's a known pedophile or a rapist. Or ICE wants to, but the judge won't do it. The whole dang system is convoluted."

I ask why they think that is. "Maybe Obama needs the black market going," responded Murray. "If the black market is cranking, well then, everybody kind of does okay. But you stop the black market, and this economy would crater.

"They've been packing drugs through here a long time, but thirty years ago, they weren't hauling nearly the drugs they are now. Now they're bringing four or five fifty-pound bundles at a time. What worries us isn't the mule, but the *pistolero* that walks behind, in case of an ambush. We kinda got a problem here with two cartels using the same mountains. La Línea and El Chapo's Sinaloa cartel. One group sits on a hill and watches a trail for packers. They'll go down and put these guys on their knees with guns to the back of their heads. Steal the drugs. Scare them back to Mexico. The *pistoleros* guard from behind, to get the drop on the other guys."

I ask them if they'd feel any safer behind Trump's proposed wall. "I don't think Donald Trump is going to build a thirty-foot wall," said Murray. "You can't build a wall high enough to keep them out. Mexico knows what a cutting torch is. Those people aren't stupid at all. They'll build a gate with hinges on it. Either that, or cut it up and haul it off for scrap metal. What Trump is going to do, needs to do, is man the border."

Judith jumped in, to clarify they have a Christian compassion for the people surviving off the cross-border drug economy. "I can't get mad at these guys that are humping these big old heavy packs. They're desperate down there. They've got a socialistic country. There's no jobs, no industries. Working for two dollars a day. They have to feed their families, and if that job is available, I don't blame them at all. There's no way for a poor person to get a leg up and get started, unless it's in the mafia. I feel we should take the job away from them, but I don't know what I'd do to feed my family."

I tell them their empathy for poor migrants doesn't seem to mesh with Trump's iron-fisted and racially inflammatory border rhetoric. "I think Trump has a lot of empathy for the Mexican people," said Murray. "When he said the Mexicans coming over are rapists and drug dealers, well, he's pretty much right, as far as the people that are going to *stay*. The Democrats are reading into what he said, because I could see myself saying the same thing. These packers humping fifty pounds of marijuana, they're throwing it down on a highway and going back to Mexico. The guys coming to stay, I think we *do* have a big mix of bad guys coming across.

"Robert Krentz, a rancher friend of ours, was killed six years ago," continued Murray. "Wasn't five miles from here. We had a guy kidnapped over here who was working on a pipeline. There was three trucks hauling drugs. Two of them got stuck in the mud. They took his pickup and made him go all the way to Wilcox, Arizona. After unloading the drugs, they said, 'If you tell them who we are or where we went, we'll come back and give you your wife's head in a paper bag.' He was really traumatized by that. Another one that's still under investigation. It could have been any of us."

"We had a big meeting in March," said Judith. "It was in Animas. Six hundred people showed up. That's a lot of people.

It was all about securing the border. Violent incidents keep happening."

"We're tired of politicians telling you stuff and doing nothing," said Murray. "We met with Senator [Martin] Heinrich a couple of weeks ago [one of New Mexico's two Democratic senators]. He's smooth. He smiles at you, tells you what you want to hear. Then he drives off. Nothing. Absolutely nothing. The only guy that's been good and consistent is Representative Steve Pearce. But he's one of many in Congress. The East doesn't understand the West. They just don't get what it's like out here. There's people back east that think the border is secure. Obama told them it is! Their attitude is, 'What do you want, a moat with alligators in it?' Well, yeah, that might help [*laughs*]! It would slow them down a little, till the alligators got full. A rancher friend of ours in Arizona, Ed Ashurst, just wrote a book called *Alligators in the Moat*. I could have written that book."

I ask them about their experiences with Border Patrol. "Border Patrol has got me to where I'm almost an anarchist," said Murray. "They've run my cattle out of the corral with their helicopters. Run my mules through barbed-wire fences. One time, it was three-thirty in the morning, they shined the brightest light I've ever seen in our bedroom window. Then hovered it over our front yard. I go out there, and they spotlight me on the porch in my BVDs. After the helicopter left, they called and said, 'This is so-and-so with the Border Patrol. We're working your area.' I said, 'No shit, Sherlock [*laughs*].' I told them, 'I almost shot your damn helicopter down, I didn't know who it was!' Boom. Here comes the FBI. They're investigating me because they said they landed the chopper to look for bullet holes. I was standing out there in my underwear, no place to hide a gun.

"If you talked to a hundred people along the border, you'd hear similar stories about Border Patrol. It's the attitude they give them in school. They hired so many, whoever could pass the test, guys from New York City and Chicago. You get to thinking about these guys when you see tattoos up to their jaw. And they're federal officers? They hold dominion over me? They tell them the people out here are probably all drug runners. Why else would we live here? Ranchers are suspects until proven guilty. If never proven guilty, you're always a suspect. Once, at a checkpoint, the agent asked if my AR-15 was fully automatic. I said, 'That's against the law, you dummy!' It's aggravating, they're looking for anything. They've been up here at night, gone through our out buildings.

"One day a helicopter came low over the windmill, scared one of my colts into a barbed wire. I had to sew up his chest. I went to Border Patrol in Deming. They locked the doors, wouldn't talk to me. Finally, a ranch liaison comes out, asks me, 'Is it true you said that if the helicopter had landed, you'd have whipped that pilot's ass?' He had a recorder in his pocket. He was trying to set me up for threatening a federal officer. I said, 'You know, I don't remember saying that, but if I would have thought of it, I'd have said it.'"

"A lot of our friends around here won't go near Border Patrol," added Judy. "Sometimes [they do] things just to make sure everybody understands they're the bosses, and we're the peons."

"One more story," said Murray. "A friend of ours was checking waters on his land, south side of Highway 9. A patrolman parks in front of him, wouldn't move. He rolls up and bumps the bumper of the Border Patrol, just to get that guy's attention. It's his ranch, his road, and here's this federal officer thinks he owns the world. Another patrolman arrives, they have him at gunpoint, lay him flat on the ground, handcuffed. Kept him that way for three hours in a hundred-and-five heat. Bumping the car—that was 'assault of a federal officer.' Border Patrol dropped the charges, but state police pursued it. It's called 'stone garden money.' The federal dollars that Border Patrol spreads to local law enforcement on the border. It buys loyalty. If the sheriffs don't do what the Border Patrol wants, they pull the 'stone garden' funds."

I pointed out that they sounded more heated when talking about the Border Patrol than they did talking about the cartels. While the Keelers grew up with Mexicans and occasional violence on the border, the kind of federal power represented by Border Patrol seems more of a foreign presence in the land. Toward the end of my day with the Keelers, Murray reminisced about his charmed youth on the old wire-fence border, where he worked and socialized with the *braceros* on his father's farm.

"I learned Spanish as a kid working with the *braceros*," he recalled. "We had fourteen *braceros* that worked for my dad's farm, halfway between Columbus and Deming. They would get in the back of our pickup and we'd take them to town to buy whatever they needed, food, clothes, and shoes. They were great guys, you know, heck. At eight years old I was introduced to tractor work. A Case Tractor with a big old clutch. The *braceros* would take me in the evenings on that same Case Tractor to putt around and shoot rabbits. The border was nothing like it is now. If there were three or four *braceros* that wanted to go home, I'd just load them in my pickup, a .22 or something hanging in the back, and just drive across the border. I'd park, go drink a beer, and come back across. Nobody ever questioned. In Deming we both went to school with Mexican kids who'd come up from Puerta Palomos. Mothers came up and had the babies at the hospital.

"The *bracero* program was a wonderful program. Bring it back. The secret on the border is, if you bring back a work program for agriculture workers, then all you have to do is enforce the law. Just enforce the law. There would be no running around trying to deport people, because they wouldn't have jobs. They'd go home by themselves. Nobody would have to deport them."

After hearing their stories, I decided to show them the route my phone had mapped to the nearest gas station. I was running low, and could think of better places to be stranded than a rocky, no-signal road in the middle of the Peloncillos.

"It's a good thing you asked," said Judith Keeler. "You don't want to go that way. It's longer and less safe. If you run out of gas or bust a tire on the rocks, nobody's coming along to help. Go the way you came in. And come back sometime after the rains. It's dry now and it looks sad. But when it's green, and the mountains are in flower, and the springs are running water, this place here is as good as it gets."

Chapter Six

California

O range County created the Orange Candidate. The Rhode Island–sized sliver of Southern California coast has served as the Right's suburban laboratory for more than half a century, exporting its products along a continental conveyer belt that connects the land of Sleeping Beauty Castle with that of Trump Tower and points in between. The citizen-scientists who built this laboratory were a myriad lot—white flighters from Los Angeles, defense industry execs from back east, conservative replants from the farm and Bible belts—but together they sent enough ideological beakers spuming to become known as, in the famous designation of *Fortune* magazine, "nut country." By the early 1960s, Orange County was establishment shorthand for the New Right that took human form in the Golem-piloting-the-Hindenburg candidacy of Barry Goldwater. Four years later, those same "nuts" were gobbling boycotted California grapes in celebration of the triumph of Richard Nixon, who developed the themes of his "silent majority" campaign, according to historian Lisa McGirr, on a close study of Orange County. Nixon wasn't alone in his regard for the place. Ronald Reagan said Orange County was "where good Republicans go to die."

Donald Trump has never been a "good Republican," but there'd be poetry in his checking into an Orange County hospice. Orange County hatched and refined the beta strains of his campaign's xenophobic nationalism, from John Birch Society anti-communism, to backlash border politics, to the "Birther" movement launched by Orange County dentist Orly Taitz. There's yet more Orange-tinted Trumpism in the county's distinction as among the largest ever to declare Chapter 9 bankruptcy.

Like the rest of the country, Nixon's Orange County has changed. Today half of the once overwhelmingly white county's residents are immigrants; a third are Latino, clustered around Anaheim and Fullerton. In April, when street clashes erupted outside a Trump rally in Anaheim—home of Disneyland, the "happiest place on earth"—Orange County protestors might have been as numerous as those from bordering L.A. County. The protests and confrontations continued the next day outside and inside Anaheim City Hall, where the city council heard arguments on a resolution denouncing Trump's rhetoric on Muslims, immigrants, and refugees. The council rejected it by a three-to-two vote.

If it were possible to program and bring to life a *Weird Science*–style prototype of the perfect California Trump voter, he or she would combine aspects of the old and new Orange Counties. He would be a white, non-religious small-business owner with working-class origins, influenced by the area's conservative-libertarian ethos, while nonetheless reflecting its changing demographics and lifestyles.

This is the profile of Kris Wyrick, a thirty-eight-year-old Trump fan with a long red goatee, shaved head, and an easy, reclined SoCal demeanor. I met Wyrik and his wife Becky in Alpine, a town of fifteen thousand nestled inside the Cuyamaca Mountains, two hours south of Anaheim. Alpine marks the beginning of eastern San Diego County, a mountainous region of isolated ranches and Border Police compounds that eventually opens into the flatter, more Mexican-flavored Imperial County and Coachella Valley. The Wyricks aren't from here. They grew up a few blocks away from each other in a Latino-majority neighborhood in Anaheim. They hopped the bus to Alpine in 2006 with two backpacks and a shared desire to get away from bad situations in Orange County. "The cops were looking for me because my mom falsely accused me of robbing her place," said Kris. "I got my backpack and I just bumped out."

Together, Kris and Becky have since built up a busy welding and repair business called Alpine Motorsports. In a giant open-air garage strung with American and Gadsen flags, Kris works on a clutter of dirt bikes, ATVs, skid loaders, and chainsaws. On weekends, he sometimes joins a local Minutemen organizer named Bob Maupin on armed citizen patrols of the border. Among his customers and friends is Republican Congressman Duncan Hunter, whose district covers east San Diego County. An immigration hardliner known for his efforts to deny federal funding to "sanctuary cities," Duncan was the first congressman to endorse Trump and lobby for his campaign on Capitol Hill.

A week before the California primary, I drank Pepsis with Kris and Becky outside their garage. We talked about their lives in Orange and San Diego Counties, race, the border, and Trump. Throughout the conversation, a brown pit bull named Kayoss eyed me warily from her bed.

"It was get out of Orange County, die, or prison," said Kris. "All my friends are in prison or dead. My ex–old lady, she's a drug addict. My son—we just needed to get away. This town saved our lives. We planted roots. Slowly but surely, we've just grown and grown. It's weird, because the majority out here is white people. [Back home], it's almost all Hispanic and you are literally fighting to stay alive. There wasn't very many of us in the neighborhoods where we grew up, around Santa Ana and Anaheim. It's all Mexican. In Garden Grove, they're all Oriental. You just try to find people that you can hang out with.

"Growing up, I got shot at. When I walked through some neighborhoods, I had to duck into bushes because of my skin color. You're walking along, all of a sudden, they're hanging out the car with guns. Happened a lot. We'd be walking around Knott's Berry Farm [an Orange County amusement park founded by conservative Nixon supporter, Walter Knott], a car pulls up, full of Mexicans, and they're like, 'What's up, wood? [*Slang for white boy.*] What the fuck you doing in my neighborhood, wood?' I've been pistol whipped, got scars here from that. . . . I've been through some shit. Sometimes trouble follows you."

Becky, who is a little younger than Kris and wears her blonde hair pulled back in a ponytail, said: "This is Orange County. When people hear 'Orange County,' they think of ritzy places like Huntington Beach, the show *The O.C.* They think of Mickey Mouse. But you go two streets over from Disneyland, you're in straight ghetto. When I used to do bad things, I'd get my drugs a block from Disneyland. There's a lot of tweakers in Orange County. Don't dare go out at night by yourself. I wouldn't go back into my old neighborhood. Last time I was in Orange County, I did drive through, but I wouldn't get out of the car. It's crazy.

"My school, Anaheim High School, was ninety-seven percent Hispanic. If you're white, you're always an outcast. For a while, I tried to fit in. I did the big hair, the lip liner. Then you get made fun of for trying to be a *chola*. So you hang out with white people, because you're accepted. But now you're a racist because you only hang out with white people. Either way, you're an outcast. I begged my mom to switch schools. She wouldn't do it. I ended up dropping out right before I graduated. I couldn't handle it. When my older friends graduated ahead of me, I was left by myself. I'd get picked on all the time: 'Oh, you don't speak Spanish? Why not? Are you racist?' I was, like, 'No, I'm not racist. My mom's not Spanish. We didn't learn it. What do you want me to do?' That's not saying I didn't have any Mexican friends. I did have.

"You're going to get stuck if you don't get the fuck out of there. Your friends ain't going to do it for you. They're only going to keep bringing you down. Alpine saved us. Gave us a chance to break away from all the nonsense. When I was growing up, I never went to the same school for two years in a row. Our kid's been in the same school district since elementary. That, to me, is fundamentally the shit. To me, that's cool. We didn't want him to have the same challenges we did. His school is pretty diverse. There's two schools here: one near the [Viejas Indian] reservation, it's a terrible school, known for raucousness. He goes to the charter in Spring Valley. It's diverse, a nice mix of everybody. He plays football, gets good grades. The black guys call him 'White Chocolate' [*laughs*]. He's accepted. That's how it should be. I saw this show on seals. They kicked out a red-headed seal from their pod. Made him live by himself because he was ginger. You got to have a good mix. That way, no one's singled out."

Kris said, "Racial profiling? Dude, I know exactly what that means. People think white people don't get racial profiled. We get racial profiled all the time. Even down here. When we first got to Alpine, we didn't have much money. We were driving a junky Jeep and got pulled over on a weekly basis. The police are, like, 'Where are you coming from, [*a local bar known for bikers and meth*]?'"

Becky said, "Kris's got the tattoos, the shaved head, the goatee. He shaves his head because he's got curly-ass hair like Richard Simmons. I got profiled, too. As a kid, walking to school, I was the only white girl in the neighborhood, so the cops thought I must be messing around. They searched me and told me to put my head back. They're looking at my eyes, asking, 'Why are your eyes shading?' I'd say, 'Because I'm looking up into the sun.' They'd search my whole bag and everything. Walking to school."

I ask them about life near the border and their experience with migrants and smugglers. "We live on a group ranch a little set back from the border," said Kris. "Our landlord has a few people on 160 acres, different houses, farm hands, stuff like that. It's a big change from the city, living on grids, block by block. We have people tramping through the back yard, but it's not as bad as out [farther east] where [Minutemen leader] Bob [Maupin] lives. When we first moved in, our neighbor told us, you ever see any Mexican comes through here, send him to my house. He helps the Mexicans out. He's been living there thirty years. He's not from here. He's still got Baja, Mexico plates on his car. But his kids were born here and they go to the school. He raises roosters for cock fighting.

"Something has to be done. Sometimes, I [join Bob] and walk the border with my gun. It may be small, but we try to do our part. Bob's been doing it a long time. His property faces south on the border. It's right there. He's had death threats. I'll do what I can. Border Patrol agents are told it's a catch-and-release thing now. Sometimes, even when it's obvious, when we catch some dude on the border with a backpack and buckets of water—Border Patrol don't respond to our calls. You'd think they might want to check this guy. What if this dude is a murderer, on his way to commit a crime? I know not everybody jumping is a murderer. But what if?"

Becky doesn't want me to get the wrong idea. "We're not against immigrants," she said. "America was built on the backs of immigrants. Nobody except the natives are from here. But we're in serious trouble. We can't keep taking everybody. How can we help anybody when we're $19 trillion in debt? I'm talking about foreign aid as well. The more people who come here, who aren't from here, who don't assimilate, you lose the country. The only reason they're here is for money. They don't want to be Americans. There's no national pride. When people don't care about the country, how can we make it better?"

Kris suggested the nation's days as a melting pot are over, or at least deserving of a new scrutiny, something you hear often talking to Trump supporters. It's a position that can rest uneasily and immediately alongside an appreciation of one's own immigrant roots.

"Obviously, let's not make it too hard," he said. "I want people to come in. This is a country of immigrants. But we're a little bit past that. Yeah, we need to shut the door slightly, stem the flow a little bit. Let's get people in here that want to work. Let's get people in here that's going to have pride for the country. You know, like citizenship classes. Let's figure out what makes this country great. I want you to understand, if you're coming into my country, what makes this country great. The freedoms you're entitled to, the things you're entitled to. Bring your history all you want, but understand that this is my country, and the path to citizenship should require that. If they're criminals, they shouldn't be here. If they have a criminal record, they shouldn't be here. You know what they do in Mexico when those motherfuckers jump the fence? They shoot them. I'm not saying that we shoot them, but you really want to talk shit on *our* border policies? Amnesty, 'safe cities', shouldn't be offered. Illegal alien means illegal alien, whether they're from Mexico or Canada. The Middle East. Can't let those guys in either. That scares the hell out of me. You don't know where they're from. They got kids over there blowing themselves up. Women that are blowing themselves up. You just don't know. I'm not a conspiracy theorist, but there's some shit going down.

"I get it. There's a lot going on in Mexico and the [Central American] countries. But you come over here, don't be like, 'Mexico! Mexico! Mexico!' Why don't you go back to Mexico and make Mexico great? Don't bring a shithole over here. Come on. I'm not going to Europe, like, 'You guys are doing it wrong, you need to have a bunch of guns over here.' That's how they do shit there. We don't really have an idea on how to fix the problem, but there is a problem. Let people come over the right way. Our friend Joe's wife is native from Mexico."

"She's Venezuelan," said Becky.

"Whatever. Wherever she's from. She went through the proper channels to get her citizenship. It was right around that time that Obama did that amnesty. [*In 2014, Obama bestowed temporary legal status and work permits on five million undocumented immigrants.*] She was so mad. She was, like, 'I went through so much stuff. I went through classes. I paid thousands. It took me forever to get it, and I finally got it.' It was just a smack in the face for the people that are actually trying to do it the proper way."

When I first met Kris and Becky a few days earlier, they had mentioned plans to join some friends and hold Trump signs opposite the entrance of a Bernie Sanders rally in San

Diego, heckling attendees the way protestors do at Trump rallies. I ask Kris what happened.

"I was gonna go, but my tooth is killing me. I didn't get no sleep last night. I don't want to go to a rally and be the guy that fights everybody. The attitude I have right now, I'll go down there and fight. What I really want to do is smack people upside the head with blunt force knowledge. I want to tell them, 'There's not enough money.' Bernie keeps saying, 'Free Free Free.' But where this money's coming from? The stuff he says about free trade? I'm down, man. I just can't handle a socialist. You can't keep giving it away. What's a college education if it's free? It ain't worth shit. Kids, back in the days, they used to work hard, they used to do things to get ahead. Mow the lawn. Our son is sixteen, has two jobs. He works here and he works at the feed store because he likes animals. That sense, it's not there anymore. It's frustrating.

"Trump is waking up the grass roots, the people that haven't voted. They're like, 'Fuck, you took our jobs!' Everybody's getting pushed out. The production jobs are gone. Now coal's under fire. You can't keep getting rid of jobs and bringing people in. There's this dilution of American pride. All the fundamental rules that America was established on, like 'One Nation Under God', you don't have that anymore."

"This is coming from a guy with a few pentagrams on his body," interjected Becky. "We are in no way, shape, or form religious."

"I don't care if you're gay, or any of that stuff," Kris continued. "I don't care if you're black, brown, yellow. I don't give a fuck. Just make your own money. Make money so that the government can get richer off of collecting taxes. The government handouts are tidbits of money, enough to keep them in that loop, but it almost forces people to do illegal things to supplement. They can't get a job, because they'll lose the benefits. So maybe they sell drugs to get what that they need.

"I'm the perfect example of coming from nothing. Moved up here with some clothes. I didn't ask anybody for help. Nobody gave me any help. I didn't take it from the government. I didn't ask for food stamps. I didn't ask for any assistance. I just did. Because there was no other way. People have that power within them."

* * *

From Alpine, I drove southeast down to Old Highway 80, a two-lane road that tracks the border and was for decades the only artery between San Diego and Georgia. In the early decades of the last century, the 80 incubated a string of thriving towns that fed off the railroad and early automobile traffic. Constant flooding caused the railroad to be relocated north in the 1920s. When the I-8 freeway was completed in the early 1970s, the Greyhounds stopped coming through, and the towns along the old 80 collapsed. All that's left along the borderlands of east San Diego County is a few VFW bars, two-star motels built on hot springs, and sleepy general stores. The bulletin boards outside these general stores all feature the same handful of fliers: a monthly barn dance, a new Mountain Women meet-up, a ranch hand offering work for living quarters, a missing man last seen in Slab City, a desert squatter's community in neighboring Imperial County.

The political spine of Old Highway 80 bends conservative, reflecting a population of ranchers like Bob Maupin, aging veterans, and part-timers and retirees from San Diego and Orange Counties. Most residents live within sight if not spitting distance of the fence that runs along most of the 187 miles of California-Mexico border. The fence was built by the second George W. Bush administration under growing pressure from Congress, where Republicans found themselves targeted by a grassroots movement that contained more than a drop of Orange County blood. Construction of the twenty-one-foot steel fence began with the signing of the 2006 Secure Fence Act. It replaced the rusted triple-wire fence that had defined the US-Mexico border for as long as anybody alive could remember. The Bush fence was taller than the old fence, but remained more political gesture than physical barrier: easily scaled, full of holes, and mute on the subject of proliferating cross-border tunnels.

Trump supporters on California's border scoff at Bush's Maginot Line in the sand. But this doesn't mean they think any more of Trump's promised Wall—the "big, beautiful wall" that is the central symbol of his "America First" campaign. The people here take the Wall as a metaphor. They assume his advisors will educate him on what they see as self-evident truth: to staunch cross-border traffic, the solution required is basic, the determining factor not tons of concrete and steel, but boots on the ground, backed by executive will.

"We don't need more wall," said Stuart Mills, a forty-eight-year old Trump supporter with a shaggy head of blonde-gray hair who owns twenty-four acres of land on Tierra del Sol Road, just off Old Highway 80. "In Europe, they have border roads. Every 100 yards, there's a guard station with machine guns, walkie-talkies, and a port-o-potty. The truck drops you and your partner off. You sit and watch. It's effective. You ain't getting across that border."

I met Mills on his property while walking the dirt roads of Boulevard, a remote and dispersed border community of three hundred souls. A contractor with a local utility company, Mills bought the land as a borderland getaway in 1997. He lives in San Diego and spends weekends and holidays here with his teenage son. Mills is a close student of border politics and its history. He is likely among the few Trump voters in the country whose friends include both Mexican smugglers as well as Border Patrol brass.

"I know a guy that smuggles people," Mills told me as he handed me a Budweiser. We were sitting on rocks overlooking the Bush fence and the mountains of Baja beyond. You could see clear for miles.

"I work with him on power lines. His family is old mafia from Mexicali. He's proud of it. He tells me everything, the routes, the schemes. He tells me straight up, 'You guys in the United States don't get it. You are brought up to work and earn, but you don't know what it's like in these countries. There is no money.'"

He pointed at the fence, tiny down below. "They just come right through here," he said. "They just use ladders, or dig under it." Then he pointed into the distance at the mountains of Baja. Nestled into one of these mountains, several miles away in Mexican territory, was a complex of some sort. "That's a prison," he said. "Border Patrol has telescopes that can see what's going on inside the prison yard. They see prisoners get executed. They stand them out there, and *Boom.* Firing squad. It's Mexico justice. My smuggler friend was in that prison for almost two months. His dad was able to buy him out."

I asked him if it's difficult balancing friendships with smugglers and support for Donald Trump. "Yeah it is," he said. "He's been caught, he's on the list, he's done prison time. You know."

We drank in silence for a minute before Mills tried to explain the ethical foundations of his border politics. "What a lot of people don't know is that illegals are modern-day slaves. Most come from El Salvador, Guatemala. They get the shit pounded out of them all the way through Mexico. How do they have $10,000 to get across? The traffickers work them to pay it off. Once they work the shit out of you for a year, year and a half, you're free. Fieldwork, roofing, digging ditches. There are 'stash houses' all through to El Centro [in California's Imperial County] with up to a hundred people sleeping on cots, pooping in one bathroom. Once that debt is paid off, they'll go get his brother or cousin, bring him across. Now he owes $10,000. . . ."

I ask Mills if he's witnessed much violence. "I heard a girl getting raped in the back part of my property one night. Screaming bloody murder. I took my gun and went looking. All of the sudden I don't hear anything. It's pitch black out here. I don't know if there are thirty of them, or what. Sometimes I see them dump the migrant [groups] out on the road. A van pulls up, kicks them out. There's seven of them, but the pick-up car has room for three. They fight trying to get in the car. The four losers start running around, they don't know where to go. Once they're here, they want to get to LA, not hang in San Diego.

"I'll tell you a story. About eighteen years ago, I was down there at the lake with my son's mother and a friend." He points beyond view into the hills below us. "She was sunbathing nude. My buddy had just bought a Thompson .45 caliber [fully automatic machine gun] and we were shooting. Out of nowhere comes this piece of shit Toyota Corolla through the bushes. No road or anything. These guys get out, and go, 'Hey, what's up?' I go, 'Fuck, I didn't think there was a road back here.' He goes, 'Aw, nah, there's no road. We make our own road.' These were big, scary dudes. Out by the lake, there's nobody. One of them looks over at my girlfriend, and goes, 'You mind if we take turns on her?' My buddy Dave goes, 'Aw, you don't want to do that . . . ' and he pulls his Thompson. They go, 'Oh, okay, you got one of those.' They pop their trunk and point two TEC-9s at us. I go, 'Oh, fuck, you don't want her, she ain't going to be into that. She scratches and shit.' I try to change the subject, and ask what they're doing. He goes, 'Oh, we're bringing some pot across. This corridor here belongs to me and my family.' We've been using it for thirty years.' I said, 'Well, how do you get across the border check down at Buckman Springs?' He goes, 'We pay people. Do you want to do a drop for us at Ocean Beach?' By that time, my girlfriend was putting her clothes on. I'm giving her looks, like, 'We got to go.' I'm looking around for anybody. There's nobody around. True story. That was under Clinton.

"Back then, we saw Border Patrol every couple of days. One agent for the entire area. Under Bush, we started getting a lot more Border Patrol. At first, they weren't welcome. They were a bunch of yahoos, driving their 4X4s through our fences and shit. People started putting spikes in their driveways, but that didn't work because they were going, 'These are government vehicles. Pop our tires, we don't give a shit [laughs].' Yeah, there was a bunch of dicks in Border Patrol, guys that couldn't be cops and now they're federal, getting into bar fights. These days it's a more professional element.

"When I first got here in '97, this abandoned town was the Wild West, drugs coming into the house through the tunnels, trafficking all over the place. What happened was— you see down where the [abandoned] railroad signs and the crossings are? The train would stop right there. In the old days, this was called 'High Pass.' It was a real flowing town. Jacumba, Boulevard, Campo, they were vacation places for everybody in Palm Springs and Imperial County. They'd come up here for the summer to get out of the heat. You can see old pictures of Jacumba with hundreds of Model Ts. When they invented air conditioning, people stopped coming. The smugglers turned the town into a haven, the houses, the old school building, they were pickup places. They all burned down five years ago in a fire. The Indians over at the [Campo] reservation got a hold of some military tracer rounds. Shot one into a bush. The winds picked up and houses burned all the way to Jacumba. My neighbor died watching a Chargers game asleep on the couch. What are you going to do? I don't go over to the reservation. I heard you get your ass kicked [*laughs*]."

I ask about corruption in the Border Patrol. "Everybody I know that brings drugs across the border says, 'You just pay the Border Patrol.' There's a bunch of corrupt Border Patrol, on both sides. But most want to do their jobs and love their country. It's a dangerous job. We've had a couple field agents killed.

"But there's a lot of ways to get drugs across besides bribes and tunnels. Listen to this—it's pretty clever. You know those little kids with squirt bottles washing car windows while you wait on the Mexican side of the checkpoint? Smugglers hand these kids a buck and say, 'Use these squirt bottles.' These bottles have [marijuana] shake in the water. The kids start squirting the car ahead of you. This sets the dogs off, there's never more than a few dogs. Now all the agents are over there, tearing that car apart, as you just go through. You get a lot of this at the Mexicali checkpoint near El Centro. It's near a back way to L.A. through Palm Springs. There's a lot of clever techniques. Drug money transferred through Mexican Walmarts. You buy gift cards for x amount of dollars and somebody down there buys things and returns them. Pretty clever.

"We're frustrated. We're not anti-Mexican. If you're here, if you see the grief that they go through. If people heard

rapes in their back property, no one around to do anything, you know? It doesn't have to be this way. The farms
used to pick up workers every morning at El Centro. They
came to the border, stood in line, and the lettuce guy said, 'I
need sixty people for about two weeks.' You signed in, got a
badge, picked lettuce for two weeks, got paid, went back to
Mexico, then back in line again. Everybody was accounted
for. Everybody got what they needed. That system worked.
Now, you sneak in and you can't get back out. When they
did away with all of that, it created this whole fuckin' hiding-
in-the-shadows situation. Border Patrol can't go to Home
Depot and say, 'Hey, you guys got your papers?' Now they're
all fuckin' cocky: 'You can't question me.' And we get repeat
people coming back from prison.

"You don't need to reinvent the wheel. My family worked
apple orchards in Washington State. There were Mexicans up
there. When the season was over, they got on a bus and went
back to picking peaches or whatever. My grandfather had
pickers' cabins for them, you know? They stayed a week or
two, then were on their way. If they wanted citizenship, there
was a policy: you came in, you signed your papers, it took
about six months, you passed a bunch of tests, you stood
there, did the pledge, you were a citizen. They stopped all
that. They closed the door.

"Take the story of my gardener to heart, man. Edgar.
He came here from Guatemala when he was fifteen. He
knocked on my door in Lakeside, and said, 'Hey, I'm in the
neighborhood, I do gardening.' Now he's thirty-two. He's got
two Ford 1–50s. Wife and kids. He works with his cousins.
They kick ass. He's a guy with a handshake and a fair price.
He pays taxes. But he cannot get his citizenship. He's paid
thousands to lawyers. He can't even come out here. I wanted
him to run my irrigation after the fire. He said, 'I don't want

to go through that border check on I-8. I don't want to get hassled and explain this and that.' Ask people and they'll tell you, 'We don't even try anymore. Come get me. I'll pay the fine.' That's kind of the attitude now. But there is no fine. If you're Mexican, you can't be checked about anything. That's how it is.

"They're blatant about it in their rallies. [California Assemblywoman] Lorena Gonzalez, right in front of everybody, says, 'The white people are afraid because we're voting in numbers. They're getting scared because we're taking over.' Who says that? Who gets away with that? That's Hitler shit. 'Oh, well, we can't cover it, we can't put that on the news.' But some white guy says something, and they go after him.

"It's not just workers coming up through here. On the news they say, 'They're just coming here to work!' Bullshit, the Bloods and Crips of Central America are getting dumped here. Arizona is overridin' with MS-13 [Mara Salvatrucha, an international Los Angeles–based Central American gang]. They learn Aztec and Mayan in the prison system so they can't get detected. The media focuses on some poor woman and a little baby. Bull-fuckin'-shit. When Trump said, 'We gotta secure our borders,' it was beyond overdue.

"It's not about a new wall. The question is, will Border Patrol be allowed to do their job? We've got telescopes mounted in the rocks all the way to Jacumba. We see everything. But Border Patrol has their hands tied. I always wave them down and talk to them, try to keep current. Once in a while they'll let us look through the telescope. I always ask about the president, whoever it is. They tell me, 'Yeah, we just got told: no more. We're allowed one a day.' It's memos, emails, straight from the commander-in-chief.

"There are Minutemen groups here that try to help. All they do is tattle. They just call the Border Patrol. They're not out there chasing people down like *Machete* [the 2010 film by Robert Rodriguez that portrays border vigilantes as bloodthirsty rednecks.] They're a pretty positive force out here. People think, 'My God! Vigilantism!" And they're, like, 'Man, we carry water, we see them, we call the border patrol and tattle on them. That's all we're doing.' Our Border Patrol is also very humanitarian. They just round them up and drop them back at the border. But when they had Career Day about a month ago at the University of San Marcos in San Diego, the Mexicans freaked out when Border Patrol joined people from the defense industry, biotech. They ran to the head of the college: 'We feel threatened!'"

Mills's admiration for the candidate goes back decades. As a transient teenager, Mills worked in downtown Manhattan cleaning out property flips by *Art of the Deal*-era Donald Trump. "It was the '80s," he says. "We were all going to be corporate entrepreneurs. I wanted to be like him, you know? Even then, everybody loved Trump or hated him, but he kept us working on these buildings. Ten bucks an hour. Then we'd fly South Carolina to New York for ninety bucks on Trump's People's Express, you know, his airline. You could be a punk rocker living on nothing on the Lower East Side, and still get from South Carolina to New York for ninety bucks."

He never seriously considered another candidate. "They tried to push Jeb Bush down our throats [*laughs*]. I sent them back their mail with nasty notes. Then they call, I give them a piece of my mind. We're tired of the machine. Do you think those people give a fuck about the people making cars and bug lamps? They don't. We see Donald Trump as somebody that has all he needs. Donald Trump probably has places nicer than the White House. It's kind of like, why not? I love it that he's a street fighter.

"I'm almost fifty. So many of us, we have kids getting to college age. We're like, why do we have colleges full of illegals getting a free ride? We're saying, 'My kid got a 3.8 average and he's not being accepted, and this kid is automatically accepted because he's an Obama 'Dreamer' [Obama's D.R.E.A.M. Act never passed Congress and hasn't been signed into law]." Tuition that should be $8,000 is $38,000 because we're paying for all the illegals to go to college. There's frustration. You can't even say 'illegals.' Now it's pretty words like 'undocumented.'

I asked Mills about Trump's proposal to round up and deport every undocumented immigrant in the country. "One of my friends is from Mexicali, she lives down near Palmer Avenue at Imperial Beach, where there's this big banner: No Trump. No Wall. She told me she's afraid Trump will try to round everybody up. It scares her. Well, I think he shouldn't have been saying that. You can't just round up 2.5 million people. But you could figure something out. What if the employers all got fined or jail time for hiring people without documents? That would put a stop to it, period. You cut the snake's head off, right there.

"Another thing that's frustrating, my son is in seventh grade, and he's constantly being called a racist. He'll listen to us, go to school, and say, 'We should do something about the border. You don't know what the illegals go through.' He'll try and tell some of their hardship, and the other kids will go, 'You're just a racist! You and your dad are just racists!' I tell him, 'Son, it's a name, don't let it bum you out, you know? But it just sucks that if you try and bring up anything, you know, the culture pounces on you. You're like, 'When in the fuck did all of this happen?'

"In southern California, things are getting way tenser between everyone. Way more. Illegals, blacks, whites. There never used to be so much of this. We all seemed to get along better before the last eight years. I'm not going to blame the president. Maybe it's society. Maybe it's the Internet. Everybody beating each other up online. I honestly don't know."

* * *

Later that afternoon, I stop for lunch on the forsaken main drag in Jacumba, an Old Highway community of 500 people with an economy built around social security checks and a trickle of tourists drawn to the local hot springs. Opposite a row of broken and boarded-up shops is the nation's most unlikely soul-food restaurant, Jay's Southern Café, run by the Cousins family of Baton Rouge. Digging into Jay's fried fish platter, I checked my email and saw a letter from Becky Wyrick. I'd written her from New Mexico asking if she and Kris had gone to a recent Trump rally in San Diego, where protestors clashed with riot police and Trump supporters, resulting in thirty-five arrests.

"The rally was fine," she wrote. "But when we left, we were flipped off, booed, spit at, things were thrown. People blocked our path to yell 'Fuck Trump.' It was scary. Without saying anything too incriminating, Kris took care of any threat that came at the family. The few scuffles I saw were in response to [Trump supporters] being pushed, poked, shoved or other-wise mistreated by the protesters. Trump supporters were there to see their candidate speak. Anybody else was there to cause trouble. A girl I work out with works for Chula Vista PD and was there in riot gear. One protestor tried to grab her vest and pull her to the ground. The real craziness popped off behind us as we walked to the car, and we didn't see how bad it got until we checked the news the next day. I'm glad we got out of there when we did."

I thought about the scene in San Diego as I drove out of Jacumba and looked south toward the mountains in Mexico, a vista that always reminds me of the famous final minutes of *The Terminator*. In the scene, Sarah Conner is stopped for gas in her Jeep somewhere near the California-Mexico line. It's windy and she's about to leave when a boy points to some dark clouds and exclaims, *"Viene una tormenta!"* Conner asks the boy's father to translate, and he tells her, "He said, 'There is a storm coming.'" To which she responds, "I know." Conner drives off in the direction of the mountains to claps of thunder and the heavy, portentous synths of the theme. The movie ends. The future begins.

Acknowledgments

I owe David Talbot more than he knows for including me in Hot Books' inaugural class of 2016. This project pulled me out of a broke winter funk, sent me to corners of the country I'd never seen, and dropped me into the marrow of a bizarre and historic primary season. My gratitude extends to Tony Lyons and his team at Skyhorse. My travels would not have been possible without a dozen Couchsurfers from Milwaukee to Mexicali who kept me on budget by offering gratis sofas, spare rooms, and patches of rug. To my Navajo friends in Phoenix, no hard feelings about the bedbugs. Last and most, thanks to my interview subjects, who opened their schedules and homes to a random Bernie guy with coffee stains on his t-shirts, lots of questions and no media affiliation. Please remember our time together when you're assigned to guard my bunkhouse in the reeducation camps.